Judy Garton-Sprenger and Philip Prowse

with Marcelo Baccarin, Helena Gomm,
and Catherine Smith

D1400532

INSIGHTS

3

STUDENT'S BOOK

MACMILLAN

Contents

Contents

Welcome to San Francisco, and hello to all the winners of our vacation contest! I'm Carrie and I'm a journalist—I work for World2day, the website with all the latest news.

Hi, nice to meet you all. I'm from Recife in Brazil. This is my first visit to San Francisco and I can't wait to see all the sights.

Hello—I'm Jay and I'm from Chicago in the U.S. I'm having a great time here! And this is Lara.

VACATION CONTEST

Win a fantastic vacation in the U.S.A.!

WORLD2DAY

Try our quiz—choose the right answers and you could be a winner!

1 The number of states in the U.S. is
○ 40. ○ 50. ○ 60.

2 The population of the U.S. is over
○ 500 million. ○ 400 million. ○ 300 million.

3 The capital of the U.S. is
○ New York City. ○ Washington, D.C. ○ Los Angeles.

4 The home of the U.S. President is
○ the White House. ○ the Pentagon. ○ the Empire State Building.

5 The longest river in the U.S. is
○ the St. Lawrence. ○ the Mississippi. ○ the Missouri.

Send

WELCOME

Hello, I'm Ramón and I live in Guadalajara in Mexico. I love music, and I'd love to go to a gig this week.

Hi! I'm Silvana from Argentina, and I want to meet lots of Americans. I can speak Spanish and French, but I'm going to speak English all the time in the States.

I'm Emma and I'm from Vancouver. No, I'm not American, I'm from Canada. I like shopping and there are some great markets here.

I'm Alex from Australia. This is a beautiful city—I'm going to buy a camera and take lots of pictures!

1 OPENER

Read the World2day quiz and try to guess the answers.

🎧 TRACK 1.02 **Now listen and check.**

2 READING

🎧 TRACK 1.03 **Read the dialogue. How many contest winners are there?**

3 AFTER READING

Answer the questions.

1 What is Carrie's job?
2 What is the name of the girl from Canada?
3 Who wants to go sightseeing?
4 Who wants to go to a concert?
5 Who is going to take lots of pictures?
6 Who wants to meet lots of Americans?
7 Where in Brazil does Lara live?
8 Which city is Ramón from?
9 Who can speak three languages?
10 Who loves shopping?

? WHAT ABOUT YOU?
Do you want to visit San Francisco? Why/Why not?

4 SPEAKING

Ask and answer questions about the people in the photo.

What's his/her name?

Where's he/she from?

EXTENSION
Write sentences about the contest winners.
Ramón is from Guadalajara in Mexico.

5 VOCABULARY

What nationalities are the winners? Choose from these words.

Word Bank: NATIONALITIES

American   Argentine   Australian
Brazilian   British   Canadian
French   Italian   Mexican   Spanish

Lara is Brazilian.

5

UNIT 1 MAKING FRIENDS

COMMUNICATIVE AIMS
LEARNING HOW TO...
1 Talk about regular activities
2 Describe what's happening now
3 Talk about possessions

TOPICS AND VOCABULARY
Clothes
Colors
Jobs and occupations
Tourist attractions

1 LANGUAGE FOCUS
Match the communicative aims (1–3) with the pictures (A–C).

A

Whose camera is it?

B

I go to the movies on Saturdays.

C

What's happening?

2 VOCABULARY
Put these words into categories.

skirt sweatshirt waiter firefighter T-shirt yellow red jeans green purple dress top nurse blue pilot reporter brown vet

CATEGORIES

Clothes

Colors

Jobs and occupations

3 VOCABULARY

Name the clothes.

 ①

 ②

 ③

 ④

 ⑤

 ⑥

4 LISTENING

🎧 TRACK 1.04

Listen to extracts 1–3 from Unit 1. Match them with these topics.

A An interview about personal information

B A description of regular activities

C Information about a social networking site

5 SPEAKING

Do the questionnaire with three other students.

How digital are you? Questionnaire

WHAT DO YOU DO IN THESE SITUATIONS?

① **When you want to know the time.**
Do you:
- look at your watch?
- ask someone?
- check your phone?

② **When you want to listen to music.**
Do you:
- turn on the radio?
- put on a CD?
- download a song?

③ **When you want to contact a friend.**
Do you:
- make a phone call?
- write a note?
- send a text?

④ **When you want to check the news.**
Do you:
- turn on the TV?
- read a newspaper?
- go online?

What interesting or surprising things did you find out? Tell another group.

BELIEVE IT OR NOT!

In a group of 23 people, there's a 50% chance that two people share a birthday!

1 DO YOU REALLY SPEAK CHINESE?

- Talking about regular activities
- Simple present

1 OPENER

What things do you like? What things don't you like?

2 READING

🎧 TRACK 1.05 **Read the dialogue. Which of these topics do they talk about?**

animals   food   languages   movies   school

SILVANA	Oh, Emma, look at those sea lions! I love them!
EMMA	You do? I don't like them at all.
JAY	Really? How about dogs? I love dogs.
EMMA	Dogs are OK, but cats are my favorite. We have two cats at home.
SILVANA	What else do you like, Jay? Do you like computer games?
JAY	No, I never play computer games. But I surf the Web and chat with people online.
SILVANA	What about movies?
JAY	I watch DVDs, but I don't often go to the movies.
SILVANA	I do. I go to the movies on Saturdays— after yoga.
EMMA	Oh, I do yoga too—every Tuesday. My mom teaches yoga.
SILVANA	And what languages do you speak?
EMMA	Oh, let's see—Italian, French, and Chinese!
JAY	Chinese? Do you really speak Chinese?
EMMA	Of course not. I'm kidding. It's a joke!
JAY	Oh. I know a good joke! Why do birds fly south in the winter?
SILVANA	I don't know. Why do they fly south?
JAY	Because it's too far to walk!

3 AFTER READING

True or false? Correct the false sentences.

1 Emma loves sea lions.
2 Emma likes cats more than dogs.
3 Jay doesn't watch movies.
4 Silvana goes to the movies every Tuesday.
5 Silvana and Emma do yoga every week.
6 Emma's mother teaches yoga.
7 Emma speaks Chinese.
8 Jay knows a joke about birds.

? WHAT ABOUT YOU?
Do you like cats more than dogs?
What languages do you speak?
What do you do on Saturdays?
What do you never do?

4 LISTENING

🎧 TRACK 1.06 **Listen and complete the sentences.**

WORLD 2 DAY — WINNERS

_____ does gymnastics and goes swimming every Friday.
_____ plays basketball and does karate.
_____ loves hip-hop and rap.
_____ chats online in English and Spanish.

Ramón

Alex

Lara

Silva

7 SPEAKING

Ask other students and complete the chart. You can write the questions first!

Do you play soccer every week?

Yes, I do. No, I don't.

Find someone who ...	Name
doesn't play soccer every week.	
drinks tea at breakfast.	
does yoga.	
speaks three languages.	
doesn't often watch TV.	
doesn't go to bed late.	
often calls friends.	
doesn't chat online.	

EXTENSION

Ask questions about other students.

A Does Mariela do yoga?
B No, she doesn't.

A Do Lucas and Fabian play soccer every week?
B Yes, they do.

8 WRITING

Look at the activities in exercise 7, and write sentences about what other students do and don't do.

Pedro doesn't play soccer every week.
Cristina drinks tea at breakfast.

Now write five sentences about yourself.

I play soccer every week. I don't drink tea at breakfast,
I drink coffee ...

EXTENSION

Write three true and two false sentences about another student. Can your partner guess which are false?

5 PRONUNCIATION

🎧 **TRACK 1.07** **Listen and repeat.**

/s/ chats	/z/ does	/ɪz/ watches
drinks	knows	chooses
eats	loves	finishes

Now listen and write these words in the correct column.

dances goes likes plays speaks teaches

6 GAME

Practice spelling.

A How do you spell "karate"?

B K-A-R-A-T-E.

A Correct! One point!

GRAMMAR WORKOUT

→ Grammar Practice on page 20

Complete.

Simple present
I _____ to the movies on Saturdays.
She **loves** sea lions.
Emma _____ Italian.
What languages _____ you speak?
Do you really _____ Chinese?
I _____n't often go to the movies.
She _____n't speak Chinese.

We use the simple present to describe states, routines, and regular activities.

UNIT 1

9

2 YOU'RE STANDING ON MY FOOT!

● Describing what's happening now
● Present progressive
● Relative pronouns: *who/that*

1 OPENER

Which of these things can you see in the photo?

bag   camera   guitar   hat   juggler   map   shirt   signs   sunglasses   umbrella

2 READING

🎧 **TRACK 1.08   Read the dialogue. Who can you see in the photo?**

RAMÓN   What's happening?

EMMA   Steve is telling everyone about San Francisco.

RAMÓN   Who's Steve?

EMMA   He's the tour guide. He's standing next to Lara. He's the one that's wearing a black jacket.

RAMÓN   What are Alex and Silvana doing? Oh, look, they're holding hands!

EMMA   No, they are not holding hands! She's helping him with his camera.

RAMÓN   Let me see!

EMMA   Ow! You're standing on my foot!

RAMÓN   Sorry. Hey, what's that man doing?

EMMA   Who do you mean? The juggler?

RAMÓN   No, the thin man who's standing behind the girl in the orange top. Look!

EMMA   Is he helping her?

RAMÓN   No, he isn't helping her. He's putting his hand in her bag. I think he's taking her wallet.

EMMA   Quick, let's stop him!

RAMÓN   He's running this way!

3 AFTER READING

Match the questions with the answers. There is one wrong answer.

1 Who is standing next to Lara?
2 Is Ramón wearing a jacket?
3 Are Alex and Silvana holding hands?
4 Is Silvana taking pictures?
5 Is Silvana helping Alex?
6 What is Ramón doing when Emma says "Ow!"?
7 Where is the thin man standing?
8 What is the thin man doing?

a Behind the girl.
b No, she isn't.
c Yes, they are.
d He's putting his hand in her bag.
e Steve.
f No, they aren't.
g No, he isn't.
h He's standing on her foot.
i Yes, she is.

? WHAT ABOUT YOU?

Who is the thin man? Is he really stealing the wallet? Why is he running? What happens next?

🎧 TRACK 1.09 **Now listen and see if you are right.**

4 PRONUNCIATION

🎧 TRACK 1.10 **Listen and count the syllables. Mark the stress.**

behind   camera   happening   jacket
orange   umbrella   video   wallet

■
behind   2

Now listen again and repeat.

5 VOCABULARY

Look at the photo of the group. Ask and answer questions about who people are.

Who's Emma? She's the one who's wearing a green top and black pants.

Who's Alex? He's the boy that's standing ...

Word Bank: CLOTHES

boots   dress   hat   jacket   jeans   pants
shirt   shoes   skirt   sneakers   sweater
sweatshirt   top   T-shirt

6 SPEAKING

Ask and answer questions about what people are doing.

A What's the girl in the orange top doing?
B She's watching the juggler.

7 WRITING

Write sentences describing the people in the photo. Don't write their names!

He's the one who's standing on the left, next to Steve. He's wearing a blue T-shirt and he's holding an umbrella.

Now give your sentences to another student. Can he/she guess the names?

 EXTENSION

Look out the classroom window and write about what is and isn't happening outside.

It's raining and no one is dancing in the street.

GRAMMAR WORKOUT

Grammar Practice on pages 20–21

Complete.

Present progressive
You're standing on my foot.
He's _____ a black jacket.
They're holding hands.
What _____ they doing?
_____ he helping her?
He _____n't helping her?
They _____ not holding hands.

We use the present progressive to talk about temporary events and what is happening now.

Relative pronouns: *who/that*
... the thin man **who**'s standing behind the girl ...
He's the one **that**'s wearing a black jacket.

We can use either *who* or _____ to refer to people.

3 IT'S MY SISTER'S BIRTHDAY

- Talking about possessions
- Possessive adjectives and pronouns
- Possessive 's and s'

Anna

1 OPENER

Which of these words do you expect to find in a text about a social networking site?

account breakfast cell phone e-mail address Internet jacket password text message username wallet

2 READING

🎧 **TRACK 1.11** **Read the text and check your answers to exercise 1.**

Luke

twitter 🐦 is one of the most popular social networking sites on the Internet. You can use Twitter to send very short messages (up to 140 characters or letters) in answer to the simple question: What are you doing? These messages are called tweets, and you send them via the Twitter website or via your cell phone as text messages.

It's easy to create an account. Ask for your parents' permission to sign up, choose a username and password, and give your e-mail address. Now you can send tweets—tell your friends what you're doing in no more than 140 characters. And lots of famous people are on Twitter, from Barack Obama to Miley Cyrus. Add them to your network and you can follow celebrities' lives day by day!

Rosie

Now look at the photos and read these tweets. Which message is ...?

Anna's   Luke's   Rosie's   Bill's   Teresa's   Scott's

A I'm waiting to interview Linkin Park. They're my favorite band, and I'm really excited!

B I'm writing a song about people's problems and what they can do about them. It's called You Can Get It Right— I hope you like it. 😉

C Our new play starts tomorrow. Everyone else knows their lines but I'm still trying to learn mine! 😞

Bill

D It's my sister's birthday and we're going to a great restaurant for a meal. I'm taking lots of pictures.

E I'm giving my dog Goldie a health check—she seems fine. I work with hundreds of animals, but I only have one of my own.

F My boss says I can't go on Twitter at work. But she's in a meeting, and it's my lunch break, so I'm having fun in the office!

Teresa

Scott

3 AFTER READING

Give short answers to the questions.

1 What is Rosie's favorite band?
2 What is *You Can Get It Right* about?
3 Who doesn't know his lines?
4 Whose birthday is it?
5 Where is Bill's boss?
6 Whose dog is called Goldie?

? WHAT ABOUT YOU?

Write your own tweet using up to 140 characters.

4 SPEAKING

Look carefully at the photos. Ask and answer questions about these things.

book   camera   cell phones   dog
glasses   guitar   laptop   microphone
pen   pink shirt   stethoscope

> Whose is the book?

> It's Luke's. Whose are the glasses?

> They're ...

Now ask and answer these questions.

Bill's guitar?

> Is it Bill's guitar?

> No, it isn't his. It's Anna's.

1 Luke's microphone?
2 Teresa's glasses?
3 Rosie's camera?
4 Bill's pink shirt?
5 Scott's cell phones?
6 Anna's dog?

5 PRONUNCIATION

 Listen and repeat.

break   eat   great   meal   mean
meet   plane   play   speak   take

Now write the words under /i/ or /eɪ/ in the chart. Then listen and check.

/i/	/eɪ/
eat	break

6 VOCABULARY

Match these definitions with jobs from the Word Bank.

a someone who takes pictures
b someone that performs in a play or movie
c a person who plays an instrument
d someone who writes or broadcasts news stories
e a doctor for animals
f someone in an office that helps his/her boss

> **Word Bank: JOBS AND OCCUPATIONS**
> actor   firefighter   musician   nurse
> PA (personal assistant)   photographer   pilot
> receptionist   reporter   teacher   vet   waiter

 EXTENSION
Write definitions of two other jobs. Can other students guess the jobs?

7 SPEAKING

Ask and answer questions about the people in the photos. What do they do, and what are they doing right now?

> What does Rosie do?

> She's a reporter. What's she doing?

> She's waiting to interview Linkin Park.

8 WRITING

Write about the people in the photos. Say what they do and what they're doing right now.

Rosie is a reporter and she's waiting to interview Linkin Park. They're her favorite band and she's really excited.

EXTENSION
Write similar sentences about three celebrities. Say what they do, and what you think they're doing right now.

> **Grammar Practice on page 21**

GRAMMAR WORKOUT

Complete.

Possessive adjectives		Possessive pronouns	
my	_____	_____	ours
_____	your	yours	yours
his/her/its	_____	his/hers/its	theirs

Possessive 's and s'

Singular noun	my sister's birthday
Plural noun	parents' permission
	celebrities' lives
Irregular plural noun	people's problems

4 **PERSONAL PROFILES**
● Integrated Skills

1 OPENER

Guess: What languages does Lara speak? What are her favorite colors?

READING

2 Read *Five Minutes with Lara* and complete the answers with sentences a–e.

a I listen to music.

b Portuguese, of course, and Spanish. And I'm learning English.

c That's easy. Pink and black!

d "Cool." Americans say "cool" all the time!

e That's difficult. Let me think. I know. I try to help someone every day.

🎧 **TRACK 1.13** **Now listen and check.**

3 Here are Ramón's answers to some of the same questions. Which questions?

1 Good music.

2 People that don't tell the truth.

3 I play the guitar.

4 My girlfriend. I'm looking forward to seeing her again.

5 I bike five kilometers before breakfast every morning.

FIVE MINUTES WITH... LARA

WORLD2DAY

Lara is one of the winners of the World2day vacation contest. What's she like? Find out here!

Hi, Lara. Where do you live?
In Recife in Brazil, but right now I'm staying at the Bridge Hotel in San Francisco.

What are your favorite clothes?
It depends. I often wear jeans and a sweatshirt, but I like dresses in the summer.

And your favorite colors?
1 _____

What is your favorite English word?
2 _____

What makes you angry?
People who don't listen.

What makes you happy?
Sunshine and blue skies!

How do you relax?
3 _____

What languages do you speak?
4 _____

Is there someone very important to you?
What do you mean? Do I have a boyfriend? I'm not telling you! But my mother is very important to me.

Is there something special you do every day?
5 _____

What are you reading right now?
An English book called *L.A. Winners*. It's great!

Thank you, Lara!

4 LISTENING

 TRACK 1.14 Read this profile. Then listen to an interview with Jay and correct six mistakes in the profile.

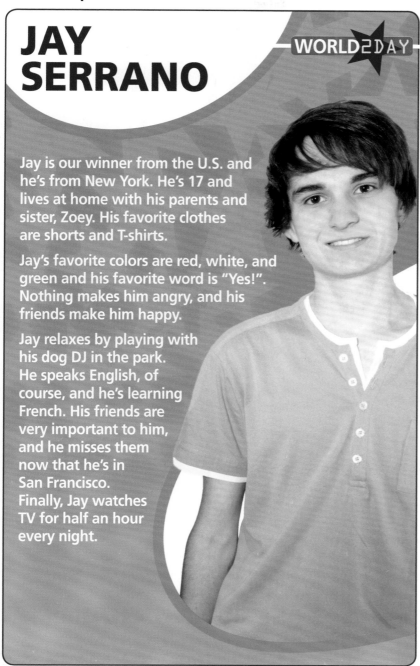

JAY SERRANO

WORLD2DAY

Jay is our winner from the U.S. and he's from New York. He's 17 and lives at home with his parents and sister, Zoey. His favorite clothes are shorts and T-shirts.

Jay's favorite colors are red, white, and green and his favorite word is "Yes!". Nothing makes him angry, and his friends make him happy.

Jay relaxes by playing with his dog DJ in the park. He speaks English, of course, and he's learning French. His friends are very important to him, and he misses them now that he's in San Francisco. Finally, Jay watches TV for half an hour every night.

5 SPEAKING

Ask another student the questions in *Five Minutes with Lara*. Note down the answers.

6 WRITING

Look at the profile of Jay. Match the information in each paragraph with the questions in *Five Minutes with Lara*.

Now write a three-paragraph profile of the student you interviewed in exercise 5.

LEARNER INDEPENDENCE

A

Different people learn in different ways. What is your favorite way of finding the meaning of a word? Put these ways in order from 1–5 (1 = best, 5 = worst).

- Use a bilingual dictionary.
- Use an English–English dictionary.
- Ask your teacher for help.
- Guess from the context.
- Ask another student.
- Use the Internet.

Now compare with another student.

B

Make your own personal phrasebook. Choose English expressions from this unit that you want to learn and write the translation next to each expression.

C

PHRASEBOOK

 TRACK 1.15 Find these useful expressions in Unit 1. Then listen and repeat.

Of course not.
It's a joke!
What's happening?
Let me see!
Ow!
Hey!
I hope you like it.
It depends.
What do you mean?

Now write a four-line dialogue using one or more of the expressions.

A *What's happening?*
B *Johnny Depp is outside.*
A *Really?*
B *Of course not. It's a joke!*

UNIT 1 MAKING FRIENDS

Insights EXTRA!

Congratulations!

LANGUAGE LINKS

When someone passes a test or is successful at something you can say "Congratulations!". Match the different ways in which people say "Congratulations!" with these languages.

French   Dutch   German   Italian   Portuguese   Russian   Spanish

Congratulazioni! Gefeliciteerd! Félicitations! Glückwünsche! ¡Felicitaciones! Parabéns! Pozdravlyayu (Поздравляю)!

You can say *Please* and *Thank you* in your language and English—what about other languages?

GAME
TWENTY QUESTIONS

- Form two teams.
- A student from Team A thinks of a celebrity.
- Students from Team B ask questions. The Team A student can answer only *Yes* or *No*.
- If they guess the celebrity with twenty questions, Team B wins a point. If not, Team A wins a point.
- Then a student from Team B thinks of a celebrity.

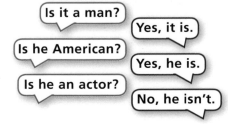

Is it a man?

Yes, it is.

Is he American?

Yes, he is.

Is he an actor?

No, he isn't.

GAME
SPELLING CHAIN

- Form two teams.
- Student 1 from Team A says and spells a word of five or more letters.
- Student 1 from Team B must say and spell a word that begins with the last letter of Team A's word.
- Student 2 from Team A continues ...
- Teams score one point for each word they spell correctly. All words must have at least five letters. If a team cannot continue, they lose a point.

Dress D-R-E-S-S

Sneakers S-N-E-A-K-E-R-S

Sister S-I-S-T-E-R

Relax R-E-L-A-X

?!?!?!

16

CONSOLIDATION

1 Look at the conversation on page 8. Write two sentences each about Silvana, Emma, and Jay using the simple present.

Silvana loves sea lions. She goes to the movies ...

2 Look at the photo on pages 10–11. Write questions and answers about what people are doing/wearing.

What's Steve doing?
He's pointing to Lara's map.

3 Make a list of clothes and other things that people wear. Use the photos on page 12 to give you ideas.

jacket, glasses, ...

4 Look at the profile of Jay on page 15. Write a similar profile of Lara using information from the web page on page 14.

Lara is our winner from Brazil, and she lives in Recife. Her favorite clothes ...

EXTENSION

1 Choose two friends or members of your family. Write sentences about:

- what they love
- what they do on weekends
- what they never do
- what languages they speak

My mother loves rock music.

2 Look at the photo in Lesson 1 on pages 8–9 and write sentences about Silvana, Emma, and Jay using the present progressive. What are they doing/wearing and where are they standing?

Emma is talking about the sea lions. She's wearing ...

3 Look at the photos on page 12. Write questions and answers about these things.

purple dress   black jacket   silver ring
blue shirt   colorful T-shirt

Whose is the purple dress?
It's ...

4 Look at Jay's profile on page 15. Write a similar profile of yourself in the third person singular.

YOUR CHOICE!

WHO AM I?

- Work in a small group.
- Think of a famous person. Write five sentences saying what the person does every day. But don't write the person's name.
- Read your sentences to the rest of the group. They try to guess who the famous person is.

WHOSE IS THIS?

- Work in a small group and use a colored plastic bag.
- Choose two small objects and put them in the bag. Don't show your objects to the rest of the group.
- One student takes objects out of the bag one by one and asks *Whose is this*?
- The other students answer *It's Diana's* or *Diana, is it yours?*

WELCOME TO THE U.S.

Ⓐ Golden Gate Bridge

There are wonderful views from this beautiful bridge, which crosses the entrance to San Francisco Bay from the Pacific Ocean. The bridge is 2.7 kilometers long, and its two towers are 227 meters tall. When it opened in 1937, it was the longest and tallest suspension bridge in the world. It's the most popular man-made tourist attraction in the U.S.

Ⓑ Walt Disney World® Resort

People travel to Florida from all over the world to visit Walt Disney World® Resort. The site in Orlando covers 121 square kilometers and has four huge theme parks with fantastic rides and lots of other attractions. Don't miss the exciting evening circus show by the Canadian company, *Cirque du Soleil*.

Ⓒ Universal's Islands of Adventure®

People also travel to Orlando to visit Universal's Islands of Adventure®. This theme park has awesome rides, exciting shows, and interactive attractions. You can meet the dinosaurs in Jurassic Park®, fly above the city streets with Spider-Man, and join your favorite American family in The Simpsons Ride™. And in 2010, a new attraction opened— The Wizarding World of Harry Potter™. The park is open 365 days a year.

Ⓓ Kennedy Space Center

Orlando vacations aren't complete without a trip to Kennedy Space Center Visitor Complex. Just east of the most popular Orlando attractions and theme parks, this is the only place on Earth where you can meet an astronaut, see giant rockets, and train in space flight simulators. The Space Center is usually open to visitors all year except on Christmas.

Ⓔ Hollywood

This part of Los Angeles is the center of the movie industry. You can take a bus tour and see the homes of up to 50 movie stars! And at the Hollywood Wax Museum, you can see models of famous people, from movie and TV stars to rock singers.

Ⓕ Niagara Falls

These world-famous falls are on the border between the U.S. and Canada. In fact, Niagara Falls are three separate waterfalls. You can take a boat trip around the bottom of the falls—boats leave every 15 minutes. You can also walk under the falls—but of course, you get wet!

Ⓖ Times Square

This New York City "square" is in fact a triangle between Broadway, Seventh Avenue, and 42nd Street. Famous for its theaters and huge advertising signs, it's always crowded with tourists. You can usually see street performers here—but be careful of pickpockets!

Ⓗ The Grand Canyon

The Grand Canyon in Arizona is probably the most popular natural attraction in the U.S. The Canyon is about 440 kilometers long, up to 24 kilometers wide, and, in some places, it's 1,800 meters deep. The south side is open all year, but the north side is only open from mid-May to mid-October because of winter snow. The Canyon gets very hot in the summer, with temperatures of up to 40°C!

Ⓘ Georgia Aquarium

Meet sharks face to face! This exciting aquarium opened in Atlanta in 2005 and has over 100,000 fish and other sea creatures. It holds 30 million liters of fresh and salt water and is the biggest aquarium in the world. It's new, it's fun, and it's open every day of the week.

⑤

⑥

⑦

⑧

⑨

1 OPENER

Look at the headings (A–I) of the U.S. sightseeing guide and try to match the places with the photos (1–9).

2 READING

Read the guide and check your answers to exercise 1. Then find the answers to these questions.

Where can you ...

1 see models of movie stars?
2 see sharks?
3 watch street performers?
4 take a boat trip?
5 see a circus show?
6 meet an astronaut?

3 VOCABULARY

Match the words with their definitions.

1 an attraction
2 an aquarium
3 a border
4 an entrance
5 a rocket
6 a triangle
7 a pickpocket

a a line between two countries
b someone who steals things from people's pockets
c a place where you can see unusual fish
d a shape with three sides
e something interesting for people to see or do
f a long thin object that travels in space
g a way into a place

4 MINI-PROJECT

SIGHTSEEING GUIDE

Work with another student and write a description of a famous place in your town/country for a sightseeing guide. Use the U.S. sightseeing guide and these questions to help you.

● Where is it?   ● What is special about it?
● What can you see/do there?   ● How old is it?   ● When is it open?

Read your work carefully and correct any mistakes. Then join other students and put your descriptions together to make a sightseeing guide.

Grammar

SIMPLE PRESENT

UNIT 1 LESSON 1

Affirmative	Negative
I/you/we/they like	I/you/we/they don't like
he/she/it likes	he/she/it **doesn't** like

Questions	Short answers
Do you/they like ...?	Yes, I/we/they do.
	No, I/we/they don't.
Does he/she/it like ...?	Yes, he/she/it **does**.
	No, he/she/it **doesn't**.

Contractions: don't = do not   doesn't = does not

- We use the simple present to describe states, routines, schedules, and regular activities:
  I go to the movies on Saturdays.
  She loves sea lions.
  Emma speaks Italian.
  What languages do you speak?
  Do you really speak Chinese?
  I don't often go to the movies.
  She doesn't speak Chinese.
- We also use the simple present to talk about what people do in their jobs and occupations:
  What does she do? (= What's her job?)
  She's a reporter. She writes news stories.
- **Spelling:** third person singular
  Most verbs add *s*:
  knows   lives   speaks
  Verbs ending in *o, ch, sh, ss, x,* and *z* add *es*:
  goes   teaches   finishes   guesses   relaxes   whizzes
  Verbs ending in a consonant + *y* change the *y* to *i* and add *es*:
  fly—flies   carry—carries
  But verbs ending in a vowel + *y* just add *s*:
  buys   enjoys   plays
  Note the irregular verb *have—**has***

PRACTICE: SIMPLE PRESENT

1 **Complete with the simple present of the verbs.**
1 Silvana _____ (love) sea lions.
2 She _____ (go) to the movies on Saturdays.
3 Emma _____ (not like) sea lions at all.
4 Jay _____ (chat) with people online.
5 He _____ (not play) computer games.
6 Emma and Silvana _____ (do) yoga.
7 _____ they _____ (see) lots of movies?
8 _____ Emma _____ (speak) Chinese?
9 Why _____ birds _____ (fly) south?
10 _____ you _____ (know) the answer?

PRESENT PROGRESSIVE

UNIT 1 LESSON 2

Affirmative	
Full forms	**Contractions**
I am helping	I'm helping
you are helping	you're helping
he is helping	he's helping
she is helping	she's helping
it is helping	it's helping
we are helping	we're helping
they are helping	they're helping

Negative	
Full forms	**Contractions**
I am not helping	I'm not helping
you are not helping	you aren't
	you're not helping
he is not helping	he isn't
	he's not helping
she is not helping	she isn't
	she's not helping
it is not helping	it isn't
	it's not helping
we are not helping	we aren't
	we're not helping
they are not helping	they aren't
	they're not helping

Questions	Short answers
Are you helping?	Yes, I am.
	No, I'm not.
	Yes, we are.
	No, we aren't.
	No, we're not.
Is he/she/it helping?	Yes, he/she/it is.
	No, he/she/it isn't.
	No, he's/she's/it's not.
Are they helping?	Yes, they are.
	No, they aren't.
	No, they're not.

- We use the present progressive to talk about temporary events and what is happening now:

  You're standing on my foot.
  He's wearing a black jacket.
  They're holding hands.
  What are they doing?
  Is he helping her?
  He isn't helping her.
  They are not holding hands.

- **Spelling:** verb + *ing*

  Most verbs add *ing*:

  hold—holding *play—playing*
  carry—carrying

  Verbs ending in e drop the e and add *ing*:

  take—taking *leave—leaving*

  Verbs of one syllable ending in a single vowel and single consonant double the final consonant before *ing*:

  swim—swimming *run—running*
  put—putting *shop—shopping*

PRACTICE: PRESENT PROGRESSIVE

2 **Write sentences using the present progressive.**

Emma/wear/black pants
Emma is wearing black pants.

1 Steve/talk/about San Francisco
2 Lara/visit/San Francisco for the first time
3 Jay and Lara/look/at the map?
4 Alex and Silvana/not hold/hands!
5 the thin man/steal/the girl's wallet?
6 Jay/hold/an umbrella
7 Silvana/watch/the juggler
8 Ramón/not listen/to Steve
9 why/Emma and Ramón/run?
10 I/not/take pictures right now

RELATIVE PRONOUNS: *WHO/THAT*

UNIT 1 LESSON 2

- We can use either *who* or *that* to refer to people:

  … the thin man who's/that's standing behind the girl …
  He's the one who's/that's wearing a black jacket.

POSSESSIVE ADJECTIVES AND PRONOUNS

UNIT 1 LESSON 3

Possessive adjectives		Possessive pronouns	
my	our	mine	ours
your	your	yours	yours
his/her/its	their	his/hers/its	theirs

- Possessive adjectives do not change with plural nouns:
  my book   ***my*** books
- We do not use *the* before possessive pronouns.
  *This book is ~~the~~ **mine**.*
- We use *Whose* to ask about possessions:
  Whose book is this? OR Whose is this book?
  Whose glasses are they? OR Whose are the glasses?

PRACTICE: POSSESSIVE PRONOUNS

3 **Complete with possessive pronouns.**

It isn't his camera. It's her camera.
The camera isn't *his* . It's *hers* .

1 This isn't your map. It's my map.
   The map isn't _____. It's _____.
2 These aren't our CDs. They're their CDs.
   These CDs aren't _____. They're _____.
3 It isn't her dog. It's his dog.
   The dog isn't _____. It's _____.
4 They aren't your books. They're our books.
   The books aren't _____. They're _____.

POSSESSIVE *'S* AND *S'*

UNIT 1 LESSON 3

- Singular nouns add *'s* (apostrophe s):
  *my sister**'s** birthday   Anna**'s** guitar*
- Plural nouns add *s'*:
  *parent**s'** permission   celebritie**s'** lives*
- Irregular plural nouns add *'s*:
  *people**'s** problems   the women**'s** bags*

PRACTICE: POSSESSIVE *'S* AND *S'*

4 **Write phrases using *'s* or *s'*.**

Emma + her cats   *Emma's cats*

1 my parents + their car
2 the teacher + her glasses
3 the children + their school
4 your doctor + his name
5 his sisters + their books
6 the people + their clothes
7 students + their work
8 Steve + his watch

UNIT 2 FESTIVALS

COMMUNICATIVE AIMS
LEARNING HOW TO...
1 Make comparisons
2 Give advice
3 Say where things are
4 Talk about likes and dislikes
5 Say what people can do

TOPICS AND VOCABULARY
Carnivals and festivals
Adjectives
Social customs
Prepositions of place
Town facilities
Music

1 LANGUAGE FOCUS

Match the communicative aims (1–5) with the pictures (A–E).

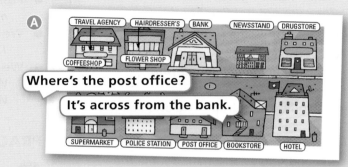

A

Where's the post office?

It's across from the bank.

TRAVEL AGENCY · HAIRDRESSER'S · BANK · NEWSSTAND · DRUGSTORE · COFFEESHOP · FLOWER SHOP · SUPERMARKET · POLICE STATION · POST OFFICE · BOOKSTORE · HOTEL

B

He's good at singing.

C

It's one of the biggest Brazilian carnivals.

D

I love going to festivals.

E

You should tell me where you're going.

2 VOCABULARY

Put these words into categories.

newsstand outside bookstore
hip-hop jazz bank behind soul
near world under
reggae salsa
hotel coffee shop
between over restaurant

CATEGORIES

Prepositions of place

Town facilities

Music

3 VOCABULARY

Match the words with the pictures.

candle

crowd

dancer

fireworks

parade

stall

4 LISTENING

🎧 TRACK 1.16

Listen to extracts 1–3 from Unit 2. Match them with these topics.

A An interview about likes and dislikes

B Information about a carnival

C A description of New Year's celebrations

5 SPEAKING

Do the *Birthday Questionnaire* with three other students.

Birthday Questionnaire

① **What do you do on your birthday?**
Do you:
- stay home or go out?
- celebrate with your friends or with your family?
- do something special or have an ordinary day?
- have a birthday party?

② **What about food on your birthday?**
Do you:
- eat at home or in a restaurant?
- eat something special? If so, what?
- have a birthday cake?

③ **What about gifts?**
Do you get gifts:
- from your family? If so, what kind?
- from your friends? If so, what kind?

④ **What happens on your ideal birthday?**

What interesting or surprising things did you find out? Tell another group.

BELIEVE IT OR NOT!

The Summerfest in Wisconsin in the United States is the world's largest music festival. It lasts 11 days and up to a million people go to it.

1 IT'S THE BEST STREET PARTY
● Making comparisons
● Comparative and superlative adjectives

1 OPENER

Talk about festivals in your country. Which are the most important? Use these words to help you.

Word Bank: FESTIVALS

band   carnival   costume   dancer   music   parade   stage   stall

2 READING

You are going to read about carnivals in Rio de Janeiro and New Orleans. Which carnival do you think is bigger? Which carnival lasts longer?

🎧 TRACK 1.17   **Now read *Carnivals* and check your answers.**

CARNIVALS

Carnival in Rio de Janeiro

In Brazil, people celebrate Carnival in February or March. Every region has its own festival, but Carnival in Rio is the most famous. It lasts four days, and millions of people go to it, including 300,000 foreign visitors. It's one of the biggest Brazilian carnivals—and it's the best, say the *cariocas* (the people of Rio).

The *escolas de samba* (samba schools) work all year to prepare for the two nights of parades in the streets and in the giant samba stadium, which holds 90,000 people. Some parades have thousands of dancers, all in the most amazing costumes, and 600 to 800 drummers. Each parade lasts 10 to 12 hours, and the judges choose the best samba school. There are also all-night carnival balls with nonstop loud samba music.

During carnival time, Rio is the most exciting city in the world, but it is also one of the most expensive—hotels and taxis cost four times as much as usual. But that's because Rio has the most spectacular carnival in the world!

Mardi Gras in New Orleans

New Orleans is recovering from the terrible effects of Hurricane Katrina in 2005. It's still a colorful cosmopolitan city, and during carnival time it's even more colorful—and noisier!

The New Orleans carnival is the largest carnival in North America, with crowds of up to a million people. It's smaller than Rio and less well known, but it lasts much longer. The New Orleans carnival season begins on January 6 with fantastic balls and exciting parties, but the main parades start two weeks before Mardi Gras ("Fat Tuesday," 46 days before Easter). There are more than 60 huge parades through the city, and there are bands playing New Orleans jazz and other kinds of music. The streets are full of people dancing in purple, green, and gold costumes. And when you get hungry, there are lots of stalls and restaurants selling exotic food.

Mardi Gras in New Orleans is the best street party in the U.S.—and it's less expensive than Rio!

3 AFTER READING

True or false? Correct the false sentences.

1 In Rio, each carnival parade lasts 24 hours.
2 During carnival time, hotels in Rio are much more expensive than usual.
3 Carnival in Rio is longer than the New Orleans carnival.
4 The New Orleans carnival starts in February or March.
5 The carnival in New Orleans is less famous than the one in Rio.
6 The New Orleans carnival is the biggest in the world.

Now read *Carnivals* again and complete the chart for Rio and New Orleans.

	Rio	New Orleans	Your festival
When?			
How long?			
How many people?			
What kind of music?			
How expensive?			
What's special about it?			

? WHAT ABOUT YOU?

Complete the chart for a festival you know about (in your country or another one).

4 SPEAKING

Look at the chart in exercise 3, and compare the two carnivals and your festival.

A The carnival in New Orleans lasts longer than the carnival in Rio.
B The carnival in my country is smaller than Rio, but it is one of the most …

5 PRONUNCIATION

 TRACK 1.18 **Listen and repeat. Then circle the /ə/ sound.**

/ə/ festiv**a**l

carnival   famous   giant   million
parade   region   samba   special
stadium   thousand

6 SPEAKING

Compare three cities in your country. Use adjectives from the Word Bank and talk about:

age   size   people   festivals   weather   sports
stores   food   attractions   atmosphere

Word Bank: ADJECTIVES

cheap/expensive   cold/hot   cool/warm   dry/wet
exciting   friendly   good/bad   old/modern
popular   quiet/noisy   safe/dangerous

A I think Puebla is older than Guadalajara.
B I think Mexico City is the oldest city in Mexico.

➡ **EXTENSION**
Play *Adjective Challenge.*

Good.   Better, the best.

Two points!

7 WRITING

Write sentences comparing cities in your country.

Guadalajara is bigger than Puebla, but Mexico City is the biggest city.

➡ **EXTENSION**
Write a paragraph for a tourist brochure about your favorite city. Say what's special about it and why it's the best place to visit.

Seattle is the coolest city in the world …

GRAMMAR WORKOUT

Grammar Practice on page 34

Complete.

Adjective	Comparative	Superlative
small	small____	the small**est**
large	large**r**	the _____
big	big**ger**	___ _____
noisy	_____	the nois**iest**
famous	**more** famous	the _____ famous
exciting	_____ exciting	the _____ exciting
expensive	**less** expensive	the **least** expensive

Irregular

good	better	___ ____
bad	worse	the worst

The opposite of *more* is _____.
The opposite of *most* is *least*.

We use comparative adjectives to compare two things.
We use superlative adjectives to compare _____ or more things.

2 WE SHOULD STAY TOGETHER

- Giving advice
- Saying where things are
- *should* and *shouldn't*

1 OPENER

What can go wrong at a festival or carnival? Think about:

crowds   food and drink
money   safety
transportation   weather

Pickpockets can be a problem in crowds.

2 READING

🎧 TRACK 1.19   **Read the dialogue. Why does Steve get angry with some of the group at the San Francisco Independence Day Parade?**

STEVE   It's a great street fair, but it's really easy to get lost here. We should stay together. Where are Emma and Alex?

JAY   I don't know.

LARA   They're dancing next to the band—in front of the Mexican food stall.

STEVE   Hey, you guys—come here! You shouldn't go away like that.

EMMA   Why not? It's a party. We're on vacation.

STEVE   You should tell me where you're going. I'm taking care of you.

EMMA   I can take care of myself. Bye!

JAY   Emma, you shouldn't go by yourself—it isn't safe. I'm coming with you!

STEVE   Now listen up, the rest of you. Stay together and meet me in half an hour at the International Coffee Shop. It's across from the movie theater. OK? Emma, Jay, come back!

3 AFTER READING

Answer the questions.

1 Who is dancing next to the band?
2 Why should they tell Steve where they are going?
3 Does Emma agree with Steve?
4 Why does Jay go with Emma?
5 When does Steve ask the others to meet him?
6 What is across from the movie theater?

GETTING IT RIGHT!
What should/shouldn't you do when …

1 … **you visit someone's home for the first time?**
   A Take flowers.
   B Arrive half an hour early.
   C Arrive a little late.
   D Take your own food with you.

2 … **you meet someone's parents?**
   A Kiss them once on the cheek.
   B Kiss them twice on the cheek.
   C Shake hands.

3 … **someone gives you a gift?**
   A Say "thank you" and open it immediately.
   B Say "thank you" and open it later.

4 … **you answer the telephone?**
   A Say "hello."
   B Say your name.
   C Say your number.
   D Say your address.

5 … **you are a guest at a meal?**
   A Start eating first.
   B Wait until others are eating.
   C Eat everything on your plate.
   D Leave some food on your plate.

? WHAT ABOUT YOU?
Do you think Emma and Jay should do what Steve says?

4 SPEAKING

Read the *Getting it right!* questionnaire. What should/shouldn't you do in your country?

5 PRONUNCIATION

🎧 **TRACK 1.20** Listen and repeat.

/s/ /ʃ/

She has sixty shirts and sixty-six skirts—she should stop shopping!

6 VOCABULARY

Look at the photo on page 26 and complete with prepositions from the Word Bank.

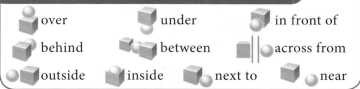

Word Bank: PREPOSITIONS OF PLACE

over	under	in front of
behind	between	across from
outside	inside	next to	near

1 Ramón is standing _____ Lara.
2 Steve is standing _____ the group.
3 Lara is _____ Ramón and Silvana.
4 Silvana is _____ Steve.
5 Jay is _____ Silvana.
6 The group is _____ the parade.

➡ **EXTENSION**

Play *What Is It?* Describe objects you can see in the classroom, but don't say their names. Can other students guess what you are describing?

> It's near the computer and over the teacher's desk.

> The clock!

7 VOCABULARY

Ask and answer questions about the town facilities.

Word Bank: TOWN FACILITIES

bank   bookstore   coffee shop   drugstore   flower shop
hairdresser's   hotel   newsstand   police station
post office   supermarket   travel agency

> Where's the bank?

> It's across from the post office.

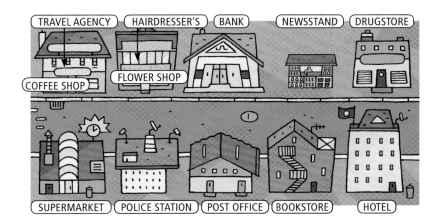

TRAVEL AGENCY   HAIRDRESSER'S   BANK   NEWSSTAND   DRUGSTORE
COFFEE SHOP   FLOWER SHOP
SUPERMARKET   POLICE STATION   POST OFFICE   BOOKSTORE   HOTEL

8 ROLE-PLAY

You are on the street in exercise 7. Act out a conversation between a visitor and a local (someone who knows the town) using these phrases.

buy some medicine
buy some stamps
find the police
book a flight
buy some flowers
get some bread
get a haircut
change some money
get a cup of coffee
buy some magazines

> Excuse me. Where can I buy some medicine?

> There's a drugstore across from the hotel.

> Thank you. And where can I ...?

➡ **EXTENSION**

Act out a similar conversation between a visitor and a local about facilities in your town.

9 WRITING

Write a paragraph giving advice to a visitor to your country. Use the topics in the questionnaire and add others.

When you visit someone's home for the first time, you should take flowers.

GRAMMAR WORKOUT

➡ **Grammar Practice on pages 34–35**

Complete.

should and *shouldn't*
We **should** stay together.
You _____ tell me where you're going.
You _____ go by yourself.
Why _____ they tell Steve?

We can use *should* or *shouldn't* to give advice.

3 **I LOVE GOING TO FESTIVALS**
- Talking about likes and dislikes
- Saying what people can do
- Verb/Preposition + gerund

FANTASTIC GLASTO!

This year's "Glasto" (as Glastonbury Festival fans call it) was better than ever. Britain's largest open-air music festival had everything: fantastic music, friendly people, and lots of mud!

Glasto is for people who love camping in the rain, like waiting in line for burgers or the bathroom, and don't mind getting covered in mud.

If you hate getting lost, make sure you don't forget your cell phone. And if you can't stand being in a crowd, then stay away. Over 150,000 people come to the festival, so you can end up a long way from the stage.

"I love going to festivals, but I hate not being able to see the band," said 18-year-old Matt from Liverpool. "So I always get up early and go to the front. The only problem is that bands often come on late—they're bad at starting on time."

Bands enjoy playing at Glastonbury. "We're not interested in earning a lot of money here," one lead singer told us. "We come for the great atmosphere and the close contact with the crowd."

Everyone wants to meet the band members, and some people are good at getting backstage. "I just smile at security," said Holly, 16, "and tell them I'm the singer's sister."

Now Glasto is over for another year, and all that's left is 200 tons of trash!

1 OPENER

Do you go to music festivals or watch them on TV? What kind of music do you like listening to?

Word Bank: MUSIC

heavy metal hip-hop jazz pop punk rap
reggae rock salsa soul techno world

2 READING

🎧 **TRACK 1.21** Read *Fantastic Glasto!* Which of these topics are in the article?

mud money music trash TV weather

3 AFTER READING

Complete.

1 Glasto fans _____ waiting in line.
2 They don't _____ getting muddy.
3 People who can't _____ being in a crowd shouldn't come.
4 If you _____ getting lost, remember to bring your cell phone.
5 Some bands are _____ at starting on time.
6 One band says they aren't _____ in earning a lot of money.
7 Holly is _____ at getting backstage.

? WHAT ABOUT YOU?

Would you like to go to a festival like Glastonbury? Why/Why not?

4 PRONUNCIATION

 TRACK 1.22 **Listen and repeat. Mark the stress.**

atmosphere   dangerous   enjoy   fantastic
festival   friendly   interested   security

■
atmosphere

5 SPEAKING

Make a list of questions beginning *Do you like ...?* and *Do you mind ...?*. Use the phrases in the box and add your own ideas. Ask two other students the questions and note down the answers.

sleep in a tent   stand up all day   listen to live music
be in a large crowd   pay a lot for a ticket
hear new bands   be a long way from the stage
wait in line for the bathroom   get covered in mud

Do you like sleeping in a tent?

Do you mind standing up all day?

EXTENSION
Write sentences about the two students you interviewed.

Fernando likes sleeping in a tent and doesn't mind standing up all day.

6 LISTENING

 TRACK 1.23   **Festival Radio interviewed people at Glastonbury. Listen and complete the chart for Holly and Matt. Use these phrases.**

dancing   getting wet   getting lost
getting up early   making new friends
meeting old friends   staying up late
talking to girls

	Holly	Matt	Another student
Loves	*meeting old friends*		
Hates			
Good at			
Bad at			

Now complete the chart for another student.

What do you love/hate doing?

What are you good/bad at?

7 WRITING

Write sentences about Holly and Matt using the information in exercise 6. Then write about the student you interviewed.

*Holly loves meeting old friends, but she hates ...
She's good at ... She's bad at ...*

 EXTENSION
Write about things you love and hate, and what you are good and bad at.

GRAMMAR WORKOUT
Complete.

Grammar Practice on page 35

Verb + gerund
I love **going** to festivals.
Bands enjoy play___ at Glastonbury.
They like _____ in line for burgers.
If you hate _____ lost ...
If you can't stand _____ in a crowd ...
They don't mind _____ covered in mud.

Preposition + gerund
Some people are good **at** get**ting** backstage.
We're not interested ___ earn**ing** a lot of money.

1 OPENER

Choose one of the photos A–F (don't say which one!) and describe it to another student. Can your partner identify the photo?

The New Year
Around the World

Here are some amazing New Year's facts!

The **Chinese** celebrate the start of the Chinese New Year in January or February, and it is the longest, the noisiest, and the most exciting holiday of the year. On New Year's Eve, all the children wear new clothes, and everyone eats special food. New Year's celebrations last 15 days, and there are dragon parades and lion dances in the streets.

In **Brazil**, people wear white clothes on New Year's Eve (December 31) to bring peace and good luck. At midnight, people go to the beach and jump over the waves seven times. Then they throw flowers into the ocean and make wishes for the new year. Some people light candles, and there are lots of parties.

One of the most unusual festivals is in **Thailand**. People celebrate the Thai New Year on April 13 with "Songkran Day". On this day, people play games with water and throw it over each other! They also visit their grandparents and ask them for good luck.

In **Japan**, most people celebrate the new year with their family. They eat special noodles on December 31, and at midnight they listen to the bells, which ring 108 times. On New Year's Day, people drink *sake*, traditional Japanese rice wine, and eat a special kind of soup. Children get envelopes with money inside, and everyone sends New Year's greeting cards.

On December 31 in **Venezuela**, people wear yellow underwear to bring good luck! At midnight, they listen to the church bells and drink champagne. Each time they hear the bell, they eat a grape and make a wish. People who want to travel in the new year carry a suitcase around the house. Other people write their wishes in a letter, and then burn it.

Like many other European countries, **Italy** celebrates the arrival of the new year with fireworks. On New Year's Eve, everyone eats lentils at a large meal that starts late in the evening and goes on even later. Some people also put lentils in their wallet or wear red clothes for good luck. Another tradition is to put a candle in the window for every member of the family.

2 READING

Read the descriptions of New Year's celebrations and match the paragraphs with the photos.

Now answer these questions.

1 Where do people eat special noodles on New Year's Eve?
2 Where do they drink champagne?
3 What do people in Brazil wear on New Year's Eve?
4 What else do people in Brazil do for New Year's celebrations?
5 Where do people eat lentils on New Year's Eve?
6 When do they celebrate the new year in Thailand?
7 How long do New Year's celebrations last in China?
8 Where are fireworks important at New Year's celebrations?

Then ask and answer similar questions.

> Where do people eat grapes on New Year's Eve?

> What do people in Venezuela wear on New Year's Eve?

3 LISTENING

 TRACK 1.24 Carrie talks about New Year's Eve in the U.S. Listen and choose the correct answer.

1 What do people often do on New Year's Eve?
  A have parties **B** go on vacation
2 What do they do at midnight?
  A go to church **B** watch a ball dropping
3 What do they do after midnight?
  A shake hands **B** sing a song
4 What do people drink?
  A champagne **B** water
5 What do they say to each other?
  A Good luck! **B** Happy New Year!

4 SPEAKING

Look at the questions in exercise 3. Ask another student about New Year's Eve traditions in his/her family.

5 WRITING

Write a paragraph about New Year's Eve in your country. Use the paragraphs in this lesson to help you. Notice that each paragraph usually:

- begins by giving the name of the country and festival, and the date
- continues by describing food and drink, and what people do
- sometimes talks about children and gifts
- uses prepositions of time: on (*date*) in (*month*) at (*time*)

LEARNER INDEPENDENCE

A

What is your favorite way of learning a word? Put these ways in order from 1–7.

- Writing the word again and again.
- Saying the word aloud again and again.
- Reviewing the word every week.
- Thinking of similar words.
- Testing yourself once a week.
- Using the word as soon as possible.
- Keeping a vocabulary notebook.

Now compare with another student. Try a new way of learning words.

B

How are your English skills? What are you good at? Assess yourself on this scale for Listening, Speaking, Reading, and Writing.

4 = Very good.
3 = Good.
2 = Not sure.
1 = Not very good.

Listening 3

Now compare with another student. Choose a skill which needs more work. What can you do to get better?

C

PHRASEBOOK

 TRACK 1.25 **Find these useful expressions in Unit 2. Then listen and repeat.**

I don't know.
Come here!
Why not?
Bye!
It isn't safe.
I'm coming with you.
Now listen up!
OK?
Come back!
The only problem is …

Now write a four-line dialogue using two or more of the expressions.

A Where's my music magazine?
B I don't know.
A Yes, you do! Come here!
B Bye!

Insights EXTRA!

PROJECT

FESTIVALS AND CELEBRATIONS

1 Work in a group and look at Unit 2 Lessons 1, 3, and 4 again. Think about festivals and public celebrations (for example, Independence Day or National Day) in your country or another country. Then choose one to write about.

2 Research: Find out information about the festival or celebration:

- What is it called? Where is it? When is it and how long does it last?
- Who goes to it? What do people do there? What kind of food is there? Is there music? What is special about it? What should you take?
- How do you get there? Where can you stay? Any problems?

3 Work together and write about the festival or celebration. Read your work carefully and correct any mistakes. Draw pictures or find photographs from magazines or online. Show your work to the other groups.

Cherry blossom festival

There are festivals all over Japan from March to May, when the cherry trees start to flower in different regions.

People have picnics with their family and friends, during the day or at night, under the *sakura* (cherry trees). They eat a special kind of sweet dish called *dango*, and they sing and play music. There are often lights on the trees at night, and that is very special. Don't forget to take your camera!

Would you like to go to a cherry blossom festival? You can get there by train—travel around Japan is easy on the *Shinkansen* high-speed trains. There are lots of good hotels, and you can also stay in a *ryokan*, a traditional Japanese inn. The only problem is choosing which of the many festivals to go to!

GAME

WRITE A POEM!

Love/Hate poem	GOOD/BAD POEM	PREPOSITION POEM
I *love* reading.	I'm good at dancing.	**Over** the crowd,
I *love* soccer.	I'm good at rap.	**Under** the stage,
I *love* fireworks.	I'm good at sleeping,	**Inside** the singer's head,
But I *hate* homework!	But I'm **bad** at writing letters!	**The song was everywhere.**
I *love* _____.	I'm good at _____.	
I *love* _____.	I'm good at _____.	*Preposition + noun*
I *love* _____.	I'm good at _____,	*Preposition + noun*
But I *hate* _____!	But I'm **bad** at _____!	*Preposition + noun*
		Sentence

Give your poems to your teacher and listen. Can you guess who wrote each poem?

CONSOLIDATION

1 Look at the chart below and write sentences comparing the three cities.

City	NEW YORK	LONDON	ATHENS
Age	400 years old	2,000 years old	6,000 years old
Population	8 million	7.5 million	3.5 million
Winter	January 4°C	January 5°C	January 9°C
Summer	July 30°C	July 18°C	July 27°C

London is older than New York, but Athens is the oldest city.

2 Look at the Word Bank for prepositions of place on page 27. Write sentences describing the position of people and things in your classroom. Use all the prepositions!

The teacher is standing in front of us.

3 Look at the chart and write sentences about Lara and Alex.

	Lara	Alex
Loves	swim	take pictures
Hates	lose things	fly
Good at	write poems	play the guitar
Bad at	get up early	dance

Lara loves swimming. She hates ...

4 Look at the text on page 30 and read the paragraph you wrote about New Year's Eve in your country. Write a paragraph about Christmas or another family celebration in your country. Think about:

food   drink   clothes   gifts   what people do

EXTENSION

1 Choose three bands, pop stars, movie stars, or sports stars and write sentences comparing them using comparative and superlative adjectives.

The Black Eyed Peas are better than Linkin Park, but I think The Strokes are the best band.

2 Write sentences about things you should/shouldn't do:

in class   on the street   at home

In class you should listen to the teacher. You shouldn't throw paper planes!

3 Choose two friends or members of your family. Write sentences about:
- what they love doing
- what they hate doing
- what they're good at
- what they're bad at
- what they're interested in

Petra loves talking to boys.

4 Write a list of questions to find out about another student's favorite festival or celebration. Then interview each other.

YOUR CHOICE!

MUSIC FESTIVAL ADVICE

Read the advice and then write sentences with *should* or *shouldn't*.

MUSIC FESTIVAL DOs AND DON'Ts
- ✔ Make sure you have enough money.
- ✗ Don't leave valuable things in your tent.
- ✔ Carry a bottle of water.
- ✗ Don't throw trash on the ground.
- ✔ Remember to take your cell phone.
- ✗ Don't take a heavy backpack.

You should make sure you have enough money.

SUPERLATIVE YOU!

- Work in pairs, but don't show each other your work.
- Complete these sentences about your partner.

  Your best time of the day is ...
  You think the greatest band in the world is ...
  Your best school subject is ...
  Your worst class of the week is ...
  Your best friend's name is ...
  Your most valuable possession is ...

- Now discuss the sentences.

  A *It says my best time of the day is the morning. That's right.*

  B *My best friend isn't Olivia. It's Toni.*

Grammar

COMPARATIVE AND SUPERLATIVE ADJECTIVES

UNIT 2 LESSON 1

Adjective	Comparative	Superlative
1 syllable		
small	small**er**	the small**est**
large	larg**er**	the larg**est**
1 syllable ending in single vowel + single consonant		
big	big**ger**	the big**gest**
hot	hot**ter**	the hot**test**
2 syllables ending in _y_		
noisy	nois**ier**	the nois**iest**
silly	sill**ier**	the sill**iest**
2 or more syllables		
famous	**more** famous	the **most** famous
exciting	**more** exciting	the **most** exciting
expensive	**less** expensive	the **least** expensive
Irregular		
good	**better**	the **best**
bad	**worse**	the **worst**

- Some two-syllable adjectives add _er/est_ or _r/st_:
  quiet   quiet**er**   the quiet**est**
  simple   simpl**er**   the simpl**est**

- The opposite of _more_ is _less_:
  It's less expensive than Rio!

- The opposite of _most_ is _least_:
  They stayed in the least expensive hotel.

PRACTICE: COMPARATIVE AND SUPERLATIVE ADJECTIVES

1 **Complete with comparative or superlative adjectives.**

1 The carnival in Rio is _____ (large) than Mardi Gras.
2 Mardi Gras is the _____ (big) carnival in North America.
3 _Cariocas_ think that Rio has the _____ (good) carnival in the world.
4 Rio is the _____ (exciting) carnival in the world.
5 It's _____ (expensive) for Americans to go to Mardi Gras than Carnival in Rio.
6 Ramón is a _____ (good) dancer than Alex.
7 Alex isn't the _____ (bad) dancer in the world!
8 The carnival in New Orleans lasts _____ (long) than in Rio.
9 The _____ (noisy) place in Rio at carnival time is the giant samba stadium.
10 People who don't have a lot of money look for the _____ (expensive) hotel.

SHOULD AND SHOULDN'T

UNIT 2 LESSON 2

- We can use _should_ and _shouldn't_ (_should not_) to express advice:
  We should stay together.
  You should tell me where you're going.
  You shouldn't go by yourself.
  Why should they tell Steve?

- _should_ is a modal auxiliary verb:
  —it does not change with _he/she/it_.
  —we use _should_ + infinitive without _to_:
  You should ~~to~~ take flowers.

PRACTICE: _SHOULD_ AND _SHOULDN'T_

2 **Read _Carnival Dos and Don'ts_. Then complete the sentences with _should_ or _shouldn't_.**

> **CARNIVAL DOs AND DON'Ts**
> ✗ Don't get lost—stay with your group.
> ✔ Walk in the same direction as the crowd.
> ✗ Don't carry lots of money.
> ✔ Keep an eye on children.
> ✗ Don't wear expensive jewelry.

1 You _____ carry lots of money.
2 You _____ keep an eye on children.
3 You _____ get lost—you _____ stay with your group.
4 You _____ wear expensive jewelry.
5 You _____ walk in the same direction as the crowd.

PREPOSITIONS OF PLACE

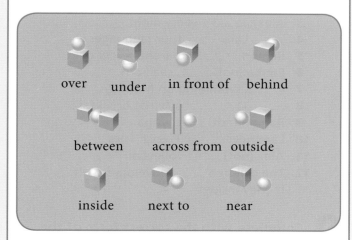

over   under   in front of   behind

between   across from   outside

inside   next to   near

- *over* is the opposite of *under*:
  There are lots of bridges **over** the river.

- *in front of* is the opposite of *behind*:
  Ramón can't see because Emma is **in front of** him.

- *outside* is the opposite of *inside*:
  You can get a taxi **outside** the station.

PRACTICE: PREPOSITIONS OF PLACE

3 **Complete with *between, in front of, next to, outside, over, under*.**

1 I can hear my phone, but I can't see it. That's because it's _____ my bed.

2 I live near the airport and planes fly _____ my house all the time.

3 My friend always sits _____ me on the bus so we can talk to each other.

4 You shouldn't sit _____ a computer for a long time.

5 It's a beautiful day. Let's go _____ and sit in the sun.

6 Ecuador is _____ Colombia and Peru.

VERB/PREPOSITION + GERUND

- A gerund (-*ing* form) is a noun formed from a verb. We can use a gerund after *love, enjoy, like, mind, hate,* and *can't stand*:
  *I love go**ing** to festivals.*
  *Bands enjoy play**ing** at Glastonbury.*
  *They like wait**ing** in line for burgers.*
  *They don't mind gett**ing** covered in mud.*
  *If you hate gett**ing** lost …*
  *If you can't stand be**ing** in a crowd …*

- We can also use a gerund after prepositions:
  *Some people are good **at** gett**ing** backstage.*
  *We're not interested **in** earn**ing** a lot of money.*

PRACTICE: VERB/PREPOSITION + GERUND

4 **Complete with the correct form of the verb.**

1 He likes _____ (be) able to see the band.

2 She's good at _____ (dance).

3 What do you hate _____ (do)?

4 I can't stand _____ (wait) for people.

5 Does she enjoy _____ (camp)?

6 They love _____ (listen) to reggae.

7 He's interested in _____ (talk) to the band members.

8 We aren't bad at _____ (speak) English!

1 Read and complete. For each number 1–12, choose word A, B, or C.

SAN FRANCISCO CELEBRATIONS

Some of San Francisco's many celebrations, like the Fourth of July (U.S. Independence Day), are very American; but others ___1___ that San Francisco ___2___ a very cosmopolitan city.

Over 100,000 people celebrate the Chinese New Year in January or February. There are lion dances, fireworks, and a huge parade through the Financial District and Chinatown. It is the ___3___ important festival of the Chinese year, and the ___4___ Asian event in North America.

Tourists ___5___ try to see the Cherry Blossom Festival at the Japan Center in April. This is a celebration of traditional Japanese culture with musicians, dancers, and artists, and a colorful ___6___.

In early May, there is a Mexican festival called Cinco de Mayo, with a carnival and lots of special events. And Carnaval San Francisco—a popular Latin American and Caribbean festival with salsa and reggae bands—___7___ on the last weekend in May.

On Independence Day there are celebrations and parties all over the city, and everyone enjoys ___8___ the amazing fireworks over San Francisco Bay.

On the night of October 31, thousands of people in costumes ___9___ to Market Street and Castro Street for a huge Halloween party. Many people think this is the ___10___ exciting night of the year.

Finally, ___11___ Christmas time, there is a huge Christmas tree in Union Square, and the stores in the square have a contest for the ___12___ store window.

1 A show	**B** shows	**C** are showing
2 A are	**B** have	**C** is
3 A more	**B** most	**C** much
4 A large	**B** larger	**C** largest
5 A should	**B** shouldn't	**C** don't
6 A dance	**B** parade	**C** walk
7 A celebrates	**B** goes	**C** happens
8 A watch	**B** to watch	**C** watching
9 A come	**B** comes	**C** are coming
10 A much	**B** more	**C** most
11 A at	**B** in	**C** on
12 A most	**B** best	**C** better

2 Complete with the correct form of the simple present of these verbs.

be   call   chat   do   drink   eat   get
go   like   play   speak   watch

1 In the evening, Silvana _____ online with her friends.
2 I (not) _____ interested in going to the movies.
3 Alex _____ TV every night.
4 _____ Lara _____ four languages?
5 Ramón _____ his parents every day.
6 Emma (not) _____ sea lions.
7 I _____ swimming on Mondays.
8 _____ Jay _____ coffee at breakfast?
9 Ramón (not) _____ yoga.
10 Lara never _____ French fries.
11 Alex (not) _____ volleyball.
12 The children _____ envelopes with money inside.

3 Complete with the correct form of the present progressive of these verbs.

help   hold   listen   make   stand   tell

1 Steve _____ _____ the group about San Francisco.
2 _____ Alex and Silvana _____ hands?
3 Silvana _____ _____ Alex with his camera.
4 _____ Steve _____ on Emma's foot?
5 The actors _____ _____ a movie.
6 _____ you _____ to me?

4 Write questions and answers.

camera/Alex
Whose camera is this? It's Alex's. It's his.

1 watch/Ramón
2 bag/Carrie
3 book/Lara
4 jacket/Steve
5 DVDs/my parents
6 sandwiches/the dancers

5 Complete with comparative or superlative adjectives.

1 The Rio carnival is _____ carnival in the world. (large)
2 Mardi Gras is _____ street party in North America. (exciting)
3 Lara is a _____ dancer than Alex. (good)
4 Jay is _____ than Emma at learning languages. (bad)
5 Who is _____ singer in the world? (popular)
6 New York is _____ city in the U.S. (big)
7 Hotels in Rio are _____ at carnival time than the rest of the year. (expensive)
8 Mardi Gras is _____ than Rio carnival. (well known)

6 **Rewrite this safety advice using *should* and *shouldn't*.**

When you go out at night ...
- Never ride with strangers, or get into a stranger's car.
- Don't stay out very late and don't walk home by yourself.
- Remember to carry a cell phone.
- Make sure you have enough money for a taxi home if necessary.
- Don't forget to check the times of the last trains and buses.

You shouldn't ride with strangers.

7 **Look at the photo on pages 10–11 and complete with these words.**

behind   between   in front of   near   next to

1 Steve is standing _____ Jay and Lara.
2 Silvana standing _____ Alex.
3 The thin man is _____ the girl in the orange top.
4 The girl in the orange top is _____ the thin man.
5 The group is standing _____ the juggler.

8 **Complete with the gerund of these verbs.**

be (x2)   dance   get   give   go   learn   wait (x2)

1 Some people don't like _____ in large crowds.
2 Lara is good at _____ to all kinds of music.
3 I can't stand _____ for people.
4 The fans don't like _____ in line.
5 Emma thinks she's bad at _____ languages.
6 Holly doesn't enjoy _____ late.
7 Silvana likes _____ to the movies.
8 Carrie loves _____ gifts to people.
9 Matt hates _____ lost.

VOCABULARY

9 **Match eight of these words with their definitions.**

candle   costume   crowd   drugstore   guide   joke
medicine   newsstand   outside   pilot   remember

1 short funny story
2 something you burn to give light
3 store where you can buy medicine
4 place where you can buy newspapers
5 opposite of *inside*
6 clothes that you wear in a play or at a carnival
7 someone who shows tourists around
8 opposite of *forget*

10 **Match the verbs in list A with the words and phrases in list B.**

	A	B
1	change	hands
2	chat	a language
3	do	online
4	get up	yoga
5	hold	games
6	make	glasses
7	play	some money
8	speak	early
9	stay at	a hotel
10	wear	a wish

LEARNER INDEPENDENCE

SELF ASSESSMENT

Look back at Lessons 1–3 in Units 1 and 2.

How good are you at ...?	✔ Fine	? Not sure
1 Talking about regular activities	☐	☐

1 I go to the movies on Saturdays.
pp74–75 exercises 2–4

2 Describing what's happening now	☐	☐

_____
pp76–77 exercises 2, 4, and 5

3 Talking about possessions	☐	☐

_____
pp78–79 exercises 2 and 5

4 Making comparisons	☐	☐

_____
p87 exercises 3–6

5 Giving advice	☐	☐

_____
p88 exercises 1 and 2

6 Saying where things are	☐	☐

_____
p89 exercise 3

7 Talking about likes and dislikes	☐	☐

_____
p90 exercises 1 and 3

8 Saying what people can do	☐	☐

_____
p90 exercise 2

Not sure? Take a look at Grammar pages 20–21 and 34–35, and do the Workbook exercise(s) again.

Now write an example for 1–8.

UNIT 3 PAST TIMES

COMMUNICATIVE AIMS
LEARNING HOW TO...
1 Talk about past events
2 Describe what was happening
3 Ask for and give reasons

TOPICS AND VOCABULARY
Buildings and places
Inventions
Transportation
Time reference words
Jobs and occupations
British English

1 LANGUAGE FOCUS

Match the communicative aims (1–3) with the pictures (A–C).

A My ears were ringing for hours afterward.

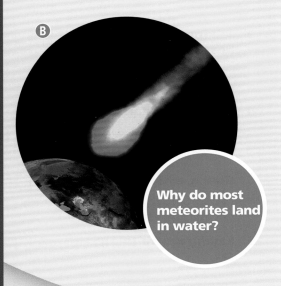

B Why do most meteorites land in water?

C The earthquake destroyed most of the city.

2 VOCABULARY

Put these words into categories.

musician helicopter evening
teacher year afternoon actor
plane doctor bus
night boat scientist
morning car day
photographer bicycle

CATEGORIES

Transportation

Time

Jobs and occupations

3 VOCABULARY

Write three more words for each of these categories.

Buildings
museum

Inventions
telephone

Verbs of movement
travel

4 LISTENING

TRACK 2.02

Listen to extracts 1–3 from Unit 3. Match them with these topics.

A A biography
B A description of a historical event
C A conversation about an accident

5 SPEAKING

Do the questionnaire with three other students.

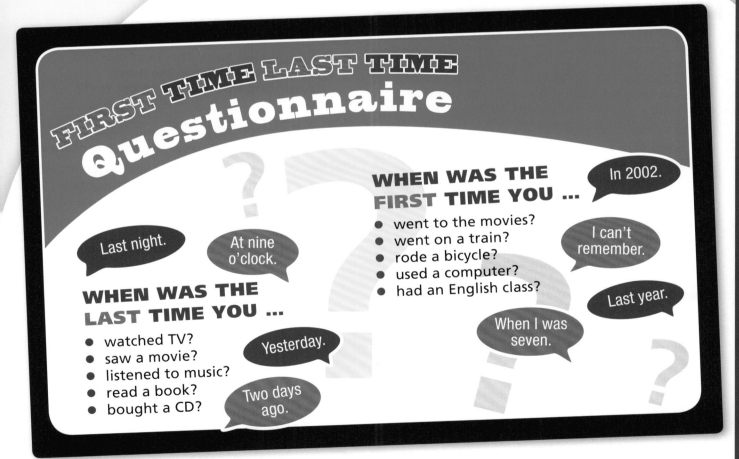

FIRST TIME LAST TIME Questionnaire

WHEN WAS THE FIRST TIME YOU ...
- went to the movies?
- went on a train?
- rode a bicycle?
- used a computer?
- had an English class?

In 2002.

I can't remember.

Last year.

When I was seven.

WHEN WAS THE LAST TIME YOU ...
- watched TV?
- saw a movie?
- listened to music?
- read a book?
- bought a CD?

Last night.

At nine o'clock.

Yesterday.

Two days ago.

What interesting or surprising things did you find out? Tell another group.

BELIEVE IT OR NOT!

The word *time* comes first in the list of most common nouns in English! Third on the list (after *person*) is *year*, and *day* is fifth.

1 A FIRE STARTED AFTER THE EARTHQUAKE

● Talking about past events (1)
● Simple past: affirmative and negative

The San Francisco Earthquake

On January 24, 1848, James W. Marshall discovered gold in a small town of 1,000 people on the coast of California. Thousands of people came to California from all over the U.S. and built the city of San Francisco. In less than 50 years, San Francisco became the largest city on the west coast, with a population of 410,000. But in 1906, the San Francisco earthquake destroyed most of the city …

The people of San Francisco were asleep when the earthquake happened at 5:12 a.m. on Wednesday, April 18, 1906. The earthquake wasn't long, only a minute, but it was extremely strong. A fire started after the earthquake and spread quickly. Everything was very dry, and the city fire department didn't have any water. People think that the fire caused 90% of the damage to the city.

The earthquake badly damaged the studio of Arnold Genthe, a photographer, and his cameras didn't work. Genthe went to a camera store and borrowed a new camera. "Take anything you want," the man in the camera store laughed. "This place is going to burn anyway."

Genthe walked around the city and took pictures of the fire. His most famous picture shows people in Sacramento Street as they watched the smoke. "Some stood and others sat on chairs," Genthe said. "When the flames came closer to them, they carried their chairs up the street. Then they sat down again."

The fire burned for four days. By the evening of Saturday, April 21, there weren't many buildings left in San Francisco. The fire destroyed 500 blocks in the downtown area, and 250,000 people lost their homes. At the time, the government reported only 375 deaths. But now people think that at least 3,000 died in the earthquake and fire.

1 OPENER

Look at the picture. Use these words to describe what you can see.

buildings   burn   chairs   flames
a hill   sit   smoke   stand   a street

2 READING

🎧 **TRACK 2.03** **Read *The San Francisco Earthquake*. What is the most surprising information in the text?**

3 AFTER READING

True or false? Correct the false sentences.

1   The San Francisco earthquake was in 1848.
2   A fire started before the earthquake.
3   The fire caused most of the damage.
4   Arnold Genthe borrowed an old camera from a store.
5   Genthe took pictures of the earthquake.
6   In Sacramento Street, some of the people sat on chairs.
7   The fire burned for five days.
8   The fire destroyed 5,000 blocks.
9   A quarter of a million people didn't have anywhere to live.
10 Now people think that at least 5,000 died.

? WHAT ABOUT YOU?

Which of your possessions would you most like to save from a fire?

4 VOCABULARY

Find the past tense of these verbs in the text. Which ones are irregular?

become   borrow   build   cause   come
destroy   die   discover   go   lose   report
sit   spread   stand   start   take   walk

5 SPEAKING

Look at the quiz and make sentences using the simple past. Then match them with the people.

> He built the first car.   Karl Benz!

QUIZ Who was the first?

1 He (build) the first car.
2 He (make) the first phone call.
3 He (be) the first person to travel in space.
4 He (make) the first cartoon movie with sound.
5 He (design) the first helicopter.
6 They (show) the first movies.
7 He (invent) the first ballpoint pen.
8 He (take) the first photograph.
9 He (print) the first book in English.

1895
The Lumière brothers

1939
Igor Sikorsky

1885
Karl Benz

1860
Antonio Meucci

1928
Walt Disney

1961
Yuri Gagarin

1826
Joseph Niepce

1938
László Bíró

1475
William Caxton

🎧 TRACK 2.04   **Listen and check. Then write sentences.**

In 1885, Karl Benz built the first car.

6 LISTENING

🎧 TRACK 2.05   **Listen and find five mistakes in the text.**

Walt Disney was born in New York in 1901 and he went to art school there. He started Walt Disney Studios with his sister on October 16, 1923. He married Lillian Bounds in 1928, and it was she who thought of the name Mickey Mouse. Disneyland, one of the world's first theme parks, opened in California on July 27, 1955. Disney planned another park in Florida, but he died on November 15, 1966 before it opened.

Now correct the mistakes in the text.

> He was born in New York.   No, he wasn't born in New York. He was born in _____.

 EXTENSION
Make more false statements about events in *The San Francisco Earthquake*.

> The earthquake was in the afternoon.   No, it wasn't! It was at 5:12 in the morning.

7 PRONUNCIATION

🎧 TRACK 2.06   **Listen and write these verbs in the correct column.**

designed   destroyed   invented
laughed   reported   showed
started   walked   watched

/d/	/t/	/ɪd/
designed	*laughed*	*invented*

Now listen and check. Repeat the words.

8 WRITING

Imagine you were in San Francisco at the time of the earthquake. Write about it in your diary! Use the text in exercise 2 to help you.

● Who were you with?
● What did you hear?
● What did you see?
● What did you do?

➡ **EXTENSION**
Think about last weekend and write answers to the questions above, including some false information. Then read your sentences to another student. Can he/she guess which are false?

GRAMMAR WORKOUT

Grammar Practice on page 52

Complete.

Simple past of *be*: was/were
Everything **was** very dry.
The people _____ asleep.
The earthquake _____n't long.
There _____n't many buildings left.

Simple past: regular verbs
The fire start__ after the earthquake.
The fire badly damage__ the studio.
They carr__ their chairs up the street.
His cameras **didn't** work.

Simple past: irregular verbs
Genthe **took** pictures of the fire.
The city fire department _____n't have any water.

Regular and irregular verbs form the negative in the same way.

2 DID YOU HAVE FUN?
- Talking about past events (2)
- Simple past: questions and short answers
- Adverbial phrases of time

1 OPENER

Read *San Francisco Facts* and match the attractions with the photos A–D.

2 READING

Read and complete the conversation with the attractions from exercise 1.

The group meets for a picnic lunch in a park.

ALEX Hi, guys. Did you have fun this morning?

SILVANA Yes, we did. It was awesome! First, we went to the ___1___.

JAY And we saw a great exhibit about the earthquake.

SILVANA Then, we took a bus downtown and went up Nob Hill to ___2___. We spent an hour there.

ALEX Did you climb up Nob Hill?

SILVANA No, we didn't. We took a ___3___. And then we went to ___4___ and visited a spectacular temple.

JAY Emma didn't. She was really lazy!

EMMA I wasn't lazy—I was thirsty! I sat outside and had a long cold drink! And the others were exhausted when they came out.

SILVANA Well, we walked a lot! My feet hurt!

EMMA And what happened to you, Alex? Were you asleep all morning?

ALEX No, I wasn't!

🎧 TRACK 2.07 **Now listen and check.**

San Francisco FACTS

- San Francisco's famous **cable car** system is a great way to get up and down the city's steep hills. You can take a cable car up Nob Hill to Grace Cathedral, and all three cable car lines go to Chinatown.
- Building work started on **Grace Cathedral** in 1910 after the earthquake. But it wasn't complete until 1964—54 years later!
- **Chinatown** is one of the world's largest Chinese communities outside Asia. It is full of stores, restaurants, and temples.
- The **California Academy of Sciences** is a large museum in Golden Gate Park, and one of its best exhibits is *Earthquake!* The museum has a multimedia theater where you can feel what it is like to be in an earthquake.

3 AFTER READING

Answer the questions.

1 What did the group do first this morning?
2 Did they see a play?
3 How did they travel downtown?
4 Where did they spend an hour?
5 Did Emma visit the temple?
6 Was she hungry?
7 Were the others tired?
8 Was Alex asleep all morning?

❓ WHAT ABOUT YOU?
Which of the places would you most like to visit? Why? Which do you think is the least interesting? Why?

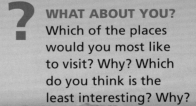

4 PRONUNCIATION

 TRACK 2.08 **Listen and count the syllables. Mark the stress.**

academy cathedral community earthquake exhausted
exhibit restaurant spectacular temple theater

■
academy 4

5 LISTENING

TRACK 2.09 **Listen to Alex and match the actions with the times.**

9:00–10:00	go to a music store
10:00–11:00	have ice cream in a coffee shop
11:00–12:00	sit in the park
12:00–1:15	surf the Internet

Now ask and answer.

A What did Alex do between nine and ten o'clock? Did he go to a music store?

B No, he didn't. He …

➡ **EXTENSION**
Play *Simple Past Challenge.*

 see   saw

6 SPEAKING

What did you do last weekend? Think about Saturday and Sunday—morning, afternoon, and night. List six different things, but don't write the times!

I went swimming. I bought some jeans.

Exchange lists with another student. Ask questions to find out when he/she did things. You can ask just 20 questions! Note down the answers.

Did you go swimming on Saturday morning? No, I didn't.

Did you go swimming in the afternoon?   Yes, I did!

7 WRITING

Write about last weekend in your diary.

*Saturday
In the morning, I went shopping and bought some jeans. At 2:30 p.m., I went swimming ...*

➡ **EXTENSION**
Read *San Francisco Facts* again and think about attractions in your town. Find out information and write one or two sentences about each of them.

GRAMMAR WORKOUT

Complete.

Simple past: questions and short answers
What **did** you do?
When ____ they go up Nob Hill?
____ you have fun?   Yes, we **did**.
Did they see a play?   No, they ____.
____ Alex asleep all morning?   No, he **wasn't**.
Were they exhausted?   Yes, they ____.

Regular and ____ verbs form questions in the same way.

Adverbial phrases of time
on Saturday (morning)   **on** August 21
in the morning   **in** August   **in** the summer
in 1910   **at** 9:00 a.m.   **at** night

➡ **Grammar Practice on pages 52–53**

UNIT **3**

43

3 IT WAS COMING STRAIGHT TOWARD HIM
- Describing what was happening
- Asking for and giving reasons
- Past progressive • *Why? Because …*

TEENAGER HIT BY METEORITE

Gerrit Blank with the mereorite that hit his hand

On June 5, 2009, Gerrit Blank was walking to the school bus when he saw a ball of light in the sky. It was coming straight toward him—a meteorite! The red-hot rock burned the schoolboy's hand and hit the ground so hard that it made a 30-cm-long hole in the road.

The meteorite crashed to Earth in Essen in Germany. Fourteen-year-old Gerrit told reporters: "I saw a large ball of light and then I suddenly felt a pain in my hand. A moment later, there was an enormous bang, like thunder! The noise was so loud that my ears were ringing for hours afterward. After the meteorite hit me, it was still falling fast enough to make a hole in the road."

Gerrit took the tiny piece of rock to school and told the story of his lucky escape. His classmates believed him. "I'm really interested in science and my teachers discovered that the rock is magnetic," he added. Experts think it was traveling at about 500 kilometers per hour when it hit Gerrit. Other experts question some of Gerrit's details but, true or not, it's a great story!

Most meteorites don't actually reach Earth because they burn up in the atmosphere. Some of them hit the ground, but most of them land in water. It's extremely rare for meteorites to hit people—the chance is about 1 in 100 million. As far as we know, there's only one other case where a person survived a meteorite strike. In November 1954, a rock crashed through the roof of a house in Alabama in the U.S. It landed on a woman, Ann Hodges, who was asleep on the sofa because she wasn't feeling well.

1 OPENER

Look at the newspaper headline and photos. Which of these words do you expect to find in the newspaper article?

atmosphere ball bridge crash escape
ground helicopter hit hole magnetic
rock roof suitcase water

2 READING

🎧 TRACK 2.10 **Read the newspaper article and check your answers to exercise 1.**

3 AFTER READING

Answer the questions.

1 What was Gerrit doing when a meteorite hit him?
2 What did he see in the sky?
3 What did he feel, and what did he hear?
4 Was the meteorite large? How do you know?
5 How fast was it traveling when it hit Gerrit?
6 Do meteorites often hit people?
7 Did the meteorite kill Ann Hodges?
8 Was she reading when the meteorite hit her?

? **WHAT ABOUT YOU?**
Do you believe Gerrit's story? Why/Why not?

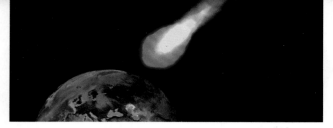

4 SPEAKING

Ask questions 1–5 and choose the correct answers from reasons a–e.

1 Why were Gerrit's ears ringing for hours?
2 Why did the meteorite make a hole in the ground?
3 Why are most meteorites magnetic?
4 Why don't most meteorites reach the Earth?
5 Why do most meteorites land in water?

a Because they contain iron.
b Because they burn up in the atmosphere.
c Because water covers more than two-thirds of the Earth.
d Because it was falling so fast.
e Because there was an enormous bang when the meteorite hit the ground.

Now write sentences with *because*.

1 Gerrit's ears were ringing for hours because ...

5 LISTENING

TRACK 2.11 Emma's brother, Ryan, had a lucky escape. Listen and decide: true or false?

1 Ryan fell overboard last month.
2 He was sailing with a friend off the coast of Africa.
3 At first the sun was shining.
4 Then the weather got better, and there was a storm.
5 It was dangerous because they were sailing in a big boat.
6 Ryan called the emergency number on his cell phone.
7 They were swimming back when the boat hit a rock.
8 A speedboat rescued them.
9 Ryan wasn't happy because he lost his watch.

Correct the false sentences. Then write a paragraph about Ryan's lucky escape.

Ryan fell overboard last year. He was sailing ...

6 PRONUNCIATION

TRACK 2.12 Listen and repeat.

/w/

Why was the white whale whistling when it was swimming in the wonderful warm water?

7 VOCABULARY

Make a word map for transportation. Use these words and add other words you know.

Word Bank: TRANSPORTATION

bicycle   boat   bus   car   helicopter   plane
rocket   ship   spaceship   speedboat   taxi   train

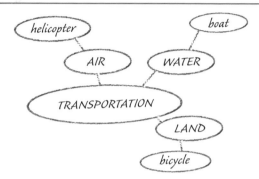

EXTENSION
Play *Word Association.*

boat   river   water   swim   fish   shark

8 WRITING

Write a paragraph about a lucky escape. Where were you? What were you doing? What happened? Why did it happen?

I was near the station. I was riding my bike to school. I almost fell off because a bus stopped suddenly in front of me.

EXTENSION
Write about what you were doing and how you felt when you heard some dramatic news.

I was playing soccer in the park when I heard about ...

GRAMMAR WORKOUT

→ Grammar Practice on page 53

Complete.

Past progressive: *was/were* + present participle
He **was** walking to the school bus when he saw a ball of light.
It _____ traveling at about 500 km/h when it hit him.
My ears _____ ringing for hours.
She _____n't feeling well.
What _____ he doing?
_____ she reading?   No, she wasn't.

We use the past progressive to say what was happening at a particular time in the past.

Why?	*Because ...* (reason)
Why was she asleep on the sofa?	She was asleep on the sofa **because** she wasn't feeling well.

4 **BIOGRAPHY**
● Integrated Skills

William Shakespeare

1 **OPENER**

You are going to read about William Shakespeare. Which of these words do you expect to find in the text?

actor exhibit meteorite
performance play playwright
roof spaceship tragedies

READING

2 **Read the text about Shakespeare and match four of these topics with paragraphs 1–4.**

Fame and fortune Marriage problems
Later life Foreign travel
Early career The first years

3 **Complete the text with these words.**

Word Bank:
TIME REFERENCE WORDS

after	between	by	finally	for	in
later	on	next	soon	until	when

🎧 **TRACK 2.13** **Now listen and check.**

4 **Answer these questions about Shakespeare.**

1 When and where was he born?
2 When did he get married? Who did he marry?
3 How many children did they have?
4 When did he start writing plays?
5 How many plays did he write?
6 What else did he write?
7 When did he die?
8 Why is he important today?

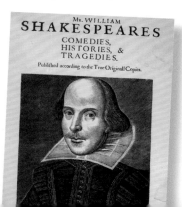

1   William Shakespeare was born __1__ April, 1564, in Stratford-upon-Avon, in the middle of England. He went to school in Stratford, and he probably became a teacher. In 1582, __2__ he was 18, he married Anne Hathaway, and they soon had three children.

2   In the late 1580s, he decided to leave Stratford and try to find work in London. __3__ this time, there were several theaters in the city—the first public theater opened in London in 1567. Shakespeare joined an acting company, and soon he was also writing plays. He quickly became a well-known actor and playwright.

3   __4__ 1589 and 1600, Shakespeare wrote about 20 plays, including *A Midsummer Night's Dream* and *Romeo and Juliet*. His plays were extremely popular, and there were even special performances for Queen Elizabeth I! Shakespeare __5__ became the most important playwright in the country. He was now a rich man, and was a part-owner of the Globe Theatre, which opened in 1599. He lived and worked in London __6__ many years, but he often went home to see his wife and children in Stratford.

4   Shakespeare's success continued into the __7__ century, when he wrote some of his most famous tragedies, including *Hamlet* and *Othello*. In all, he wrote 37 plays, and he also wrote many beautiful poems. __8__, he returned to Stratford in 1611, and he lived there __9__ he died, aged exactly 52, __10__ April 23, 1616. In his will, he left his wife his second-best bed! __11__ his death, two actor friends collected all his plays and published them in 1623. Today, 400 years __12__, he is one of the most famous writers in the world, and there are many movies of his plays.

5 LISTENING

🎧 TRACK 2.14 **Listen to a description of the life of Charles Dickens, the English novelist, and complete the chart with dates and numbers.**

Charles Dickens

Date	
February 7, _____	Born in Portsmouth, on the south coast of England.
_____	Family moved to London.
_____	Left school, started working in a factory.
_____	First novel: *The Pickwick Papers*.
1836	Married Catherine Hogarth, had _____ children.
_____	Visited the U.S. for the first time and wrote *American Notes*, which criticized slavery.
1836–65	Wrote _____ major novels, including *Oliver Twist*, *David Copperfield*, and the ghost story *A Christmas Carol*.
June 9, _____	Died suddenly after a tour of the U.S. Most popular English writer of the _____th century.
Over _____ years later	His books are still bestsellers, many movies of his novels.

6 SPEAKING

Ask and answer questions about the life of Charles Dickens. Use the questions in exercise 4 to help you.

(When was he born?) (On February 7, 1812.)

7 WRITING

Find out information about a famous person in your country: for example, a writer, a musician, or an artist. Make notes about the person's life, similar to the chart in exercise 5.

Now write four paragraphs about the person. Use some of the topics from exercise 2, and the time reference words from exercise 3.

LEARNER INDEPENDENCE

A

When you want to learn new words, you can make associations. For example, you can associate a word:

- with a picture in your mind
- with a sound or a color
- with other words in the same category
- with a word in your language
- with a person or a story

Choose some words and try to learn them by making associations.

B

Word maps are a great way to organize vocabulary. In Lesson 3 you made a word map for transportation. Now make a word map for jobs and occupations.

C

PHRASEBOOK

🎧 TRACK 2.15 **Find these useful expressions in Unit 3. Then listen and repeat.**

Did you have fun?
It was awesome!
What happened to you?
There was an enormous bang!
It's extremely rare.
As far as we know, …
She wasn't feeling well.

Now think of other situations where you could use each of the two exclamations.

"It was awesome!"
Talking about a movie.

 UNIT 3

UNIT 3 PAST TIMES

Insights EXTRA!

LANGUAGE LINKS

Read and find out what these dates and numbers refer to.

● 1604   ● 250 million   ● 1620s   ● 1475   ● 6 million

English past and present

In Shakespeare's time, around 6 million people spoke English, and they all lived in Britain. Then people emigrated to North America in the 1620s, and to Australia and New Zealand in the 1770s and 1790s. Today there are around 60 million English-speakers in Britain, almost 250 million in the U.S., 27 million in Canada, 18 million in Australia, and nearly four million in New Zealand.

Books and spelling

William Caxton printed the first book in English in 1475. In Caxton's time, different people spelled words in different ways. Caxton himself spelled *book* sometimes *booke*, and sometimes *boke*. The first dictionary appeared in 1604, but it only contained about 3,000 words. It wasn't until 100 years later that everyone agreed on how to spell English words.

How many words are there in English today?
A 10,000   **B** 100,000   **C** At least 1,000,000

GAME
LINK-UP

● Form two teams.
● One team chooses a letter square from the game board. The teacher asks a question about a word beginning with the letter. If the team guesses the word, they win the square.
● Then the other team chooses a letter square ...
● The first team to win a line of *linked* squares, from top to bottom or from left to right, is the winner. You can go in any direction, but all your squares must touch!

C	A	M	R
B	H	Q	F
W	T	P	N
D	K	S	E

CONSOLIDATION

1 Choose ten verbs from page 40, exercise 4. Write a sentence with each verb in the simple past.

Karl Benz built the first car.

2 Look at the dialogue on page 42. Write simple past questions beginning *How ...?*, *What ...?*, *When ...?*, or *Who ...?* and then answer them.

How did the group travel up Nob Hill?
They took a cable car.

3 Look at the photo on page 44. Write questions about what Gerrit was doing/wearing, and then answer them.

Was Gerrit crying?
No, he wasn't crying, he was ...

4 Imagine you are interviewing Shakespeare's ghost. Look at the Reading text on page 46 and the questions in exercise 4. Write an interview between yourself and Shakespeare's ghost.

Me: When and where were you born?
Ghost: I was born in April, 1564, in
*   Stratford-upon-Avon.*

EXTENSION

1 Write about yesterday in your diary, saying what you did and didn't do.

2 Look at the conversation on page 42 and your answers to exercise 5. Write a similar conversation between yourself and Alex.

Me: Hi, Alex! Did you have fun this morning?

3 Look back at the photo in Unit 1 Lesson 2. Write sentences about what people were doing/wearing and where they were standing.

Steve was pointing to Lara's map.
He was wearing ...

4 Look at the Reading text on page 46 and at your completed chart in Listening exercise 5. Write four paragraphs about the life of Charles Dickens.

YOUR CHOICE!

SIMPLY THE BEST!

- Work in a small group.
- Think about the best things that happened to you last week. Make a list, for example:
  At home: *the best meal I had / the best TV show I saw / the best game I played / the best song I heard / the best surprise I had was ...*
  At school: *the best class I had / the best piece of work I did / the best homework I had / the best book I read / the best website I visited was ...*
- Take turns asking and answering questions about the best things that happened last week.
A *What was the best meal you had?*
B *Spaghetti—I love pasta.*

SURVEY: TRANSPORTATION

- Work in a small group.
- Each group member interviews three other students and notes down the answers. Ask these questions:
  How did you get to school today?
  Is it the same every day?
  How did your parents get to work today?
  Is it the same every day?
  How did you travel when you last went on vacation?
  What's your favorite way of traveling?
- Now work together and use your notes to write a summary of the interviews. Compare your summary with another group.
  Today five students walked to school, three biked, six came by bus, and the rest came by car.

1 OPENER

How much do you know about New York? Try our New York quiz.

Hello New York! Quiz

1 In 1624, the first people came to live in New York from Europe. They were:

Ⓐ French   Ⓑ Dutch   Ⓒ English   Ⓓ Italian

2 New York City is on the:

Ⓐ Kennedy River   Ⓑ Times River
Ⓒ Hudson River   Ⓓ Liberty River

3 Manhattan is:

Ⓐ a forest   Ⓑ a person
Ⓒ an island   Ⓓ a river

4 The population of New York City is:

Ⓐ 6,000,000   Ⓑ 8,000,000
Ⓒ 10,000,000   Ⓓ 12,000,000

2 READING

Read *The First New Yorkers* and check your answers to the quiz. Then number these events to show the order in which they happened.

A An Italian sailed into New York Harbor.
B The English changed the name to New York.
C The Algonquian Indians lived on the island of Mannahatta.
D An Englishman discovered the Hudson River.
E A Dutchman bought Manhattan.

VOCABULARY

3 Match the words with their definitions.

1	native	**4**	explorer
2	forest	**5**	boss
3	island	**6**	nonsense

a piece of land with water around it
b something that isn't true or an idea that seems very stupid
c people who were born in the place
d person in charge at work
e someone who travels to new places to find out what they are like
f large area covered with trees

4 Match these American and British words.

American English	British English
apartment	car park
cell phone	chemist's
drugstore	chips
French fries	film
garbage, trash	flat
movie	mobile phone
parking lot	railway
railroad	rubbish
sneakers	shop
store	trainers

5 MINI-PROJECT

Town history

Work with another student and write a short history of your town. Use *The First New Yorkers* and these questions to help you.

- Where is your town?
- When did people first live there? Where did they come from?
- What was the town called at that time? Did it have the same name as now?
- What are the important dates in your town's history? Why are they important?

Read your work carefully and correct any mistakes. Then show your *Town history* to other students.

The First New Yorkers

Only a few hundred years ago, the only people to live in New York were Native Americans—the Algonquian Indians. They lived in a forest on an island which they called Mannahatta. Then Giovanni da Verrazano, an Italian explorer, discovered New York Harbor in 1524, and in 1609, an Englishman, Henry Hudson, found the Hudson River. But it was the Dutch who came to live in New York in 1624. In 1626, a Dutchman named Peter Minuit bought Mannahatta island from the Algonquian Indians for $24—today the island is called Manhattan. The Dutch name for their town was New Amsterdam, but in 1664, the English took the town and changed the name to New York after the English city of York. At that time, the population of New York was about 1,500—now there are over eight million New Yorkers!

People continued to speak Dutch in parts of New York well into the 19th century. Many words in American English came from the Dutch who lived in New York. These include: *boss, Yankee, cookie, nitwit* (= stupid person), and *poppycock* (= nonsense). The question *How come?* (meaning *Why?*) also comes from a Dutch word, *hoekom*. The grammar of British English is very similar to American English, but the vocabulary is often different. For example, *pants* are called *trousers* in British English, and in British English *pants* means underwear!

Van Nieuw Engelandt.
't Fort nieuw Amsterdam op de Manhatans

UNIT **3**   **51**

Grammar

SIMPLE PAST

UNIT 3 LESSONS 1 AND 2

be

Affirmative	**Negative**
I/he/she/it was	I/he/she/it wasn't
	(was not)
we/you/they were	we/you/they weren't
	(were not)

Questions	**Short answers**
Were you ...?	Yes, I was.
	No, I wasn't.
	Yes, we were.
	No, we weren't.
Was he/she/it ...?	Yes, he/she/it was.
	No, he/she/it wasn't.
Were they ...?	Yes, they were.
	No, they weren't.

● There are only two simple past forms of *be*:
  Everything was very dry.
  The people were asleep.
  The earthquake wasn't long.
  There weren't many buildings left.

● In questions, the subject comes after *was/were*:
  Was Alex asleep all morning?
  Were they exhausted?

Regular verbs

Affirmative	**Negative**
I	I
you	you
he/she/it started	he/she/it didn't start
we	we (did not start)
you	you
they	they

Questions	**Short answers**
Did you start?	Yes, I/we did.
	No, I/we didn't. (did not)
Did he/she/it start?	Yes, he/she/it did.
	No, he/she/it didn't.
Did they start?	Yes, they did.
	No, they didn't.

● **Spelling:** affirmative forms of regular verbs
  Most verbs add *ed*:
    start—started   destroy—destroyed
  Verbs ending in *e* add *d*:
    damage—damaged   die—died
  Verbs ending in a consonant + *y* change the *y* to *i* and add *ed*:
    carry—carried   marry—married

● Simple past negative: subject + *didn't* + infinitive without *to*:
  His cameras didn't work.
● Simple past questions: *did* + subject + infinitive without *to*:
  What did you do?
  When did they go up Nob Hill?
  Did you have fun?
  Did they see a play?

Irregular verbs

● There is a complete list of all the irregular verbs used in this book on page 127.
● Irregular verbs form the negative and questions in the same way as regular verbs:
  The city fire department didn't have any water.

PRACTICE: SIMPLE PAST

1 **Complete with the simple past of these verbs.**

buy   come   destroy   go   lose   sit   start   take

1 The students _____ down after the teacher came in.
2 He _____ all the way from Denver last night.
3 They _____ work on the cathedral more than 50 years ago.
4 The earthquake _____ part of the city.
5 We _____ to a great party last night.
6 He _____ the bus home about ten minutes ago.
7 I _____ my ID card last week.
8 She _____ some new jeans on Saturday.

2 **Complete with the simple past of the verbs. Then look back at page 42 and answer the questions.**

1 Where _____ the group _____ (go) first?
2 What _____ they _____ (see) there?
3 When _____ (be) work complete on Grace Cathedral?
4 When _____ the work _____ (start)?
5 _____ they _____ (spend) an hour in Grace Cathedral?
6 _____ Jay and Silvana _____ (climb) Nob Hill?
7 _____ (be) Emma thirsty?
8 _____ Emma _____ (have) a hot drink?
9 _____ (be) the others exhausted when they came out?
10 _____ Alex _____ (visit) the temple?

ADVERBIAL PHRASES OF TIME

UNIT 3 LESSON 2

- We use *on* for days and dates:
  on Saturday (morning)   on August 21

- We use *in* for periods during the day (except *night*), months, seasons, and years:
  in the morning   in August
  in the summer   in 1910

- We use *at* for specific times:
  at 9 a.m.   at noon/midnight

  and in certain fixed expressions:
  at night   at sunrise

PRACTICE: ADVERBIAL PHRASES OF TIME

3 **Complete the sentences with *in*, *on*, or *at*.**

1 The party ended _____ eleven o'clock.
2 We had a great time _____ Saturday.
3 The San Francisco earthquake happened _____ April 18, 1906.
4 The first Europeans came to California _____ 1542.
5 We saw the meteorite _____ nine thirty _____ night.
6 He went to the park _____ Sunday afternoon.
7 I got up early _____ the morning.
8 She was born _____ May.

PAST PROGRESSIVE

UNIT 3 LESSON 3

Affirmative	**Negative**
I/he/she/it was walking	I/he/she/it wasn't walking
we/you/they were walking	we/you/they weren't walking
Questions	**Short answers**
Were you walking?	Yes, I was.
	No, I wasn't.
	Yes, we were.
	No, we weren't.
Was he/she/it walking?	Yes, he/she/it was.
	No, he/she/it wasn't.
Were they walking?	Yes, they were.
	No, they weren't.

- We use the past progressive to describe what was happening at a particular time in the past, to give the background to an event:

- We form the past progressive with *was/were + -ing* form:
  He was walking to the school bus when he saw a ball of light.
  It was traveling at about 500 km/h when it hit him.
  My ears were ringing for hours.
  She wasn't feeling well.
  What was he doing?
  Was she reading? No, she wasn't.

PRACTICE: PAST PROGRESSIVE

4 **Look back at the photos on pages 42–43. Complete the sentences with the past progressive of the verbs.**

1 Jay _____ (not/ride) the cable car.
2 Ramón and Silvana _____ (smile) at the camera.
3 They _____ (not/look) at the ocean.
4 _____ Emma _____ (stand) next to Jay? Yes, she _____.
5 _____ Emma _____ (eat) a banana? No, she _____.
6 _____ everyone _____ (have) fun? Yes, they _____.
7 _____ Alex _____ (take) pictures? No, he _____.
8 _____ it _____ (rain)? No, the sun _____ (shine).

UNIT 3 LESSON 3

- We use the conjunction *because* to introduce clauses of reason or cause which answer the question *Why ...?*
  Why was she asleep on the sofa?
  She was asleep on the sofa because she wasn't feeling well.

PRACTICE: *WHY? BECAUSE ...*

5 **Match the questions with the answers.**

1 Why was Lara feeling happy?
2 Why were you late?
3 Why wasn't Silvana feeling well?
4 Why was Emma drinking a soda?
5 Why were Jay and Silvana exhausted?
6 Why was the museum awesome?

a Because they walked a lot.
b Because it had a great earthquake exhibit.
c Because she had a great day.
d Because she was thirsty.
e Because her feet hurt.
f Because I was asleep all morning.

COMMUNICATIVE AIMS
LEARNING HOW TO...
1 Talk about cause and effect
2 Make predictions
3 Talk about the way people do things

TOPICS AND VOCABULARY
Recorded music
Feelings
Performance
Adverbs
TV shows
Grammar words

1 LANGUAGE FOCUS
Match the communicative aims (1–3) with the pictures (A–C).

Ⓐ Actors work really hard.

Ⓑ What will replace MP3 players?

Ⓒ If we mix red and green, we get yellow.

2 VOCABULARY
Put these words into categories.

talent show
nervous
sitcom
angry
happy
afraid
noun
documentary
news
sad
verb
adjective
preposition
scared
drama
adverb
cartoon
infinitive

CATEGORIES
Feelings

TV shows

Grammar words

3 VOCABULARY

Match the words with the pictures.

artist
actor
doctor
musician
police officer
politician

TRACK 2.16

4 LISTENING

Listen to extracts 1–3 from Unit 4. Match them with these topics.

A A description of a TV series

B A description of how something works

C Instructions for a drama exercise

5 SPEAKING

Do the *Media Questionnaire* with three other students.

Media Questionnaire

① HOW MANY HOURS A WEEK DO YOU ...

- watch TV?
- listen to recorded music?
- spend online?
- play video games?

② HOW MANY TIMES A MONTH DO YOU ...

- go to the movies?
- watch a DVD?
- go to the theater?
- go to a concert?

What interesting or surprising things did you find out? Tell another group.

! BELIEVE IT OR NOT!

96.7 percent of homes in the U.S. have TVs, and American households spend an average of eight hours a day watching television—that's twice as long as anyone else!

1 IF WE MIX RED AND GREEN …

- Talking about cause and effect
- Open conditional with *if/when*

1 OPENER

Think about pictures you and your friends took during the last year. Which are your favorites?

2 READING

TRACK 2.17 **Read *How a Digital Camera Works*. Name one new fact which you learned from the article.**

HOW A DIGITAL CAMERA WORKS

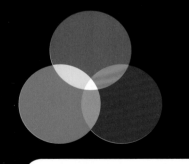

Digital cameras produce instant photos that you can print at home, share online, or send to friends from your phone. They're really simple to use— but how do they actually work?

Unlike traditional cameras, digital cameras don't use film. Instead, they have a computer chip covered in millions of tiny squares called pixels. The more pixels a camera has, the better pictures it takes. When you press the button on the camera, each pixel records the brightness of the light it 'sees'. When the camera records what it sees, it uses numbers, not images.

But the pixels only record light and dark. So do digital cameras only take black and white pictures? No, when you look at digital photos, you see color pictures. So where does the color come from?

There are three primary colors of light: red, green, and blue. What happens if we mix the three primary colors? We get white! If we mix red and green, we get yellow, and so on. This is how your eyes, a computer screen, and a digital camera work. In a digital camera, there's a filter in front of each pixel, so it 'sees' only one of the three colors.

There's also a computer in your camera that mixes the colors. When you take a picture, the computer compares what each pixel 'sees' with the other pixels around it. During this process, the computer makes millions of calculations in a few seconds.

And the great thing is that if you don't like the pictures, you can always delete them!

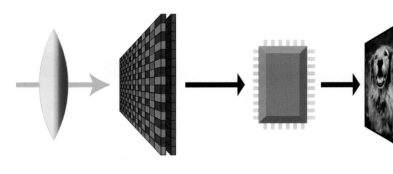

3 AFTER READING

Match the beginnings with the endings.

1 You get instant pictures
2 When you take a picture with a digital camera,
3 A digital camera uses numbers
4 When you look at digital photos,
5 You get white light
6 The computer makes millions of calculations

a if you mix red, green, and blue.
b when it records what it sees.
c they are in color.
d when you use a digital camera.
e when it compares what each pixel 'sees'.
f each pixel records the brightness of the light.

? WHAT ABOUT YOU?
What are your favorite pictures? Are they pictures of people, places, events, or things?

4 VOCABULARY

Match the words with their definitions.

compare   digital   instant   pixels
make calculations   primary colors

1 when something happens immediately
2 square on a computer chip which records light
3 recording information as numbers
4 you mix them to make other colors
5 see how things are the same or different
6 use mathematics to figure out answers

5 PRONUNCIATION

🎧 **TRACK 2.18** **Listen and repeat. Which word does not end in the sound /əl/?**

animal   capital   digital   example
hotel   impossible   middle   model
noodle   pixel   simple   special

6 LISTENING

🎧 **TRACK 2.19** **Carrie and Emma have a talk. Listen and decide: true or false? Then correct the false sentences.**

1 Emma doesn't know what to say to Jay and Ramón.
2 It's not hard for Emma to show her feelings.
3 She's usually nervous when she meets people.
4 She doesn't like it if people tell her what to do.
5 Carrie suggests that Emma sees both boys after the vacation.
6 The boys want Emma to choose one of them.

▶ EXTENSION
Tell each other what you think of Emma. What do you think she should do about her problem?

7 WRITING

Complete these statements for another student without talking to him/her. Then show them to him/her. How many did you get right? Correct the statements that are wrong.

THIS IS YOU

Your favorite song is ...
You are very happy when you ...
You don't like it when people ...
If you get into trouble, you ...
Your favorite food is ...
When you meet someone new, you feel ...
If you get angry, you ...
You feel good if you ...
Your favorite color is ...

▶ EXTENSION
Complete the statements in the chart for yourself and add five more.

GRAMMAR WORKOUT

 Grammar Practice on page 66

Open conditionals with *if/when*
If we **mix** red and green, we **get** yellow.
When you **look** at digital photos, you _____ color pictures.
What _____ if we mix the three primary colors?
When you _____ a picture, the computer compares ...

We use the open conditional to talk about cause and effect.

In open conditional sentences, both verbs are in the _____ _____ tense.

57

UNIT 4
SOUND AND VISION

2 WHICH WILL WE CHOOSE?
- Making predictions
- Simple future: *will/won't*

MUSIC TO YOUR EARS
– the history of recorded music

1 OPENER

When and where do you listen to music? Do you download it or listen to CDs?

2 READING

Match the photos 1–5 with these ways of listening to music: cassette, CD, LP, MP3 player, phonograph.

🎧 **TRACK 2.20** Now read *Music to Your Ears* and complete it with these words. Then listen and check.

Word Bank: RECORDED MUSIC

cassette tapes CDs LPs MP3 players records

3 AFTER READING

True or false? Correct the false sentences.

1 In the 19th century, cylinders were more popular than records.
2 Thomas Edison invented the tape recorder.
3 Tape recorders weren't available in the U.S. until 1948.
4 LPs became less popular after the invention of the Walkman.
5 CDs were very expensive when they first appeared.
6 Most people think that CDs will replace MP3 players.

? WHAT ABOUT YOU?

Do you have a Walkman, a record player, or another old-fashioned music player at home? Do your parents keep their old records and tapes?

4 PRONUNCIATION

🎧 **TRACK 2.21** Listen and repeat.

/ɪ/ will	/i/ we'll
live	leave
fit	feet
it	eat
sit	seat
tin	teen
fill	feel

Now listen and write the words you hear.

1877

Thomas Edison invented the phonograph, which recorded sound on cylinders. Four years later, Charles Tainter invented the first flat disc record. Which were the most popular: cylinders or records? Surprisingly, __1__ weren't popular for another 50 years. Until the 1920s, most people listened to music on cylinders on a phonograph.

1928 and 1948

In 1928, Dr. Fritz Pfleumer invented tape recording in Germany, but tape recorders weren't available in the U.S. until 20 years later. Also, in 1948, the invention of the LP (long-playing record) meant that people could hear more music on each record—around 23 minutes a side. Which did people choose: tapes or LPs? Most people chose __2__, but after Sony introduced the Walkman® in 1979, more and more people listened to __3__.

1982

Compact discs appeared in 1982. At first they were very expensive, but by the 1990s they were more popular than both LPs and cassettes. But how much longer will CDs be popular? Apple introduced the first iPod® in 2001, and more and more people bought Internet-based MP3 players.

The Future

MP3 or CD: which will we choose? Most people think that __4__ will soon replace __5__. The big question is: what will replace MP3 players? We won't know the answer to that question for a few years.

5 SPEAKING

What do you think will happen next? Choose A, B, or C.

> I think Emma will say she doesn't have any money.

> I don't agree—I think she'll say it's a great idea because she loves shopping.

1 Lara and Silvana want Emma to go shopping with them. Will Emma
  A say no because she doesn't have any money?
  B say no because she's too tired?
  C say it's a great idea?

2 Steve brings his dog to the hotel. Will Jay
  A say he's afraid of dogs?
  B say he prefers cats?
  C say he wants to take the dog for a walk?

3 It's Lara's birthday. Silvana gives her a black T-shirt as a gift. Will Lara
  A say "thank you" and then try to exchange it?
  B say she loves black?
  C say "thank you" and not wear the T-shirt?

4 Ramón is playing the guitar. Will Alex
  A start dancing?
  B start singing?
  C take some pictures?

 TRACK 2.22 **Now listen and check.**

6 WRITING

What do you think will happen to you in the future? What are your hopes? Think about travel, work, home, and relationships, and write predictions.

I'm sure I'll travel a lot, but I don't think I'll work overseas.

Now compare your predictions with other students.

EXTENSION

What do you think will replace MP3 players? How will we listen to music in ten or twenty years' time? Compare your ideas with other students.

GRAMMAR WORKOUT

Grammar Practice on page 66

Complete.

Simple future: *will/won't*
MP3 players _____ soon replace CDs.
We _____ know the answer for a few years.
What _____ replace MP3 players?
Which _____ we choose?

We can use *will/won't* to say what we predict or hope about the future.

3 YOU SPOKE TOO FAST

- Talking about the way people do things
- Adverbs of manner

1 OPENER

The group visited a movie studio and took part in a scene as extras. Look at the photo of the group. Which of these adjectives describe how they are feeling?

Word Bank: FEELINGS

afraid   angry   happy   nervous   sad   scared

Guess: What is Steve saying?

2 READING

🎧 TRACK 2.23 **Read the dialogue and check your answers to exercise 1.**

STEVE	Is everyone here? Well, I have some bad news. The director isn't going to use your scene in the movie.
JAY	Oh, that's too bad! Why not?
STEVE	She thinks you acted badly.
EMMA	I don't understand—it doesn't make sense. We weren't acting, we were being ourselves.
STEVE	I know, and I thought you were great—you did really well. But the director thinks you spoke too fast.
EMMA	That's crazy! We just spoke normally, that's all.
RAMÓN	I think it's because we didn't have enough time to rehearse properly.
STEVE	It's not just a question of rehearsing, Ramón. Actors work extremely hard—they spend hours doing drama exercises.
LARA	Can you do some of these exercises with us?
STEVE	Of course. Does everyone want to try?
ALL	Yes!

3 AFTER READING

Match the questions with the answers. There are two wrong answers.

1 Why isn't the director going to use the group's scene?
2 What does the director think about the way they spoke?
3 How did the group speak?
4 What does Ramón think the problem was?
5 How do actors spend a lot of their time?
6 What is Steve going to do with the group?

a In the way that they usually do.
b Doing drama exercises.
c They're going to rehearse the scene again.
d She thinks they spoke too quickly.
e Some drama exercises.
f Steve thinks they spoke too slowly.
g He thinks they needed a longer rehearsal.
h Because she didn't like their performance.

? WHAT ABOUT YOU?

How do you feel when you are performing in front of people—for example, acting in a role-play, playing music, doing gymnastics? Do you enjoy it? Why/Why not?

4 PRONUNCIATION

🎧 **TRACK 2.24** **Listen and write these words in the correct column.**

director everyone exercise
extremely happily normally
properly rehearsal tomorrow

▪■▪	■▪▪
director	*everyone*

Now listen and check. Repeat the words.

5 LISTENING

🎧 **TRACK 2.25** **Steve explains two drama exercises to the group. Listen and choose the correct answer.**

1 In the first exercise, Steve tells them how to run/walk/move.
2 In the second exercise, he tells them to sing/talk/play.

Now listen to the second drama exercise and guess the adverb of manner before the group does! Choose from the adverbs in the Word Bank.

1 Alex 2 Emma 3 Jay
4 Silvana 5 Lara 6 Ramón

Word Bank: ADVERBS OF MANNER

angrily happily loudly nervously
politely quickly quietly rudely
sadly slowly

➤ **EXTENSION**
Do the drama exercises using the adverbs in the Word Bank.

6 VOCABULARY

Match the definitions 1–6 with six of these nouns.

Word Bank: PERFORMANCE

actor band character concert director
drama movie musician play rehearsal
scene show stage studio theater

1 place where people make a movie or TV/radio show
2 short part of a movie or play
3 practice of a play, piece of music, etc. before a performance
4 actor's role in a movie or play
5 part of a theater where actors/musicians perform
6 person who tells the actors what to do

➤ **EXTENSION**
Write definitions of five more words from the Word Bank. Then read your definitions aloud to another student, but don't say the words. Can he/she guess the words?

7 WRITING

Write a paragraph describing a character in a movie or TV series.

● Who is the character and where does he/she live?
● What does he/she do?
● What does he/she usually wear?
● How does he/she talk and behave?
● Why do/don't you like the character?

GRAMMAR WORKOUT

Complete.

Adverbs of manner

Regular		Irregular	
Adjective	**Adverb**	**Adjective**	**Adverb**
bad	_____**ly**	early	early
normal	_____	fast	_____
proper	_____	good	_____
quick	quick**ly**	hard	hard
angry	ang**ri**ly	late	late
happy	happ**i**ly		

We use adverbs of manner to describe *how* we do something.

➤ **Grammar Practice on page 67**

UNIT **4** 61

CLASSIC TV SERIES

1 _____

The imaginary city of Springfield in the U.S. is the setting for one of the world's most successful TV series. People in over 70 countries follow the activities of the cartoon characters in *The Simpsons*, a satire of middle-class American life. Matt Groening created the Simpson family—he named Homer, Marge, Lisa, and Maggie after his own parents and sisters, and substituted Bart for his own name. The first broadcast was in 1989, and the show is now the longest-running American sitcom.

2 _____

Medical drama series are always popular, and one of the best ever is *House, M.D.*, which takes place in a hospital. It is about Dr. Gregory House and his team of doctors as they deal with accidents, emergencies, and serious illnesses. Dr. House is a genius, but his ideas and decisions are often against hospital rules, and he often has arguments with his boss, other doctors, and patients. Drama meets mystery and dark comedy in this original show.

3 _____

In *Ugly Betty*, smart, friendly Betty Suarez works in an office for a fashion magazine. She isn't pretty, and she doesn't wear fashionable clothes, but she's a really nice person. There's often trouble in the office, and Betty always helps her boss with his many problems. The first broadcast was in 1999 in Colombia—now the soap is very popular all over the world, from India to Mexico, and from Italy to Japan.

4 _____

This TV series ran on CBS from September 2011 to May 2012. The main character is a female police detective in New York, Carrie Wells. She has a very rare medical condition: *hyperthymesia*. She can remember everything visually! She says: "Pick any day of my life, and I can tell you what I saw or heard: faces, conversations, clues (which comes in handy when you're a cop)." *Unforgettable* is very popular in Europe, the Americas, Asia, Australia. Everyone is waiting for a new series!

1 OPENER

What are the names of popular TV shows in your country? What kinds of shows are they? Choose from these words. Can you think of an example of each kind of show?

Word Bank: TV SHOWS

cartoon   drama   documentary   game show   music show
news show   reality show   science fiction series   sitcom
soap (opera)   sports show   talent show   talk show   thriller

2 READING

Read *Classic TV Series* and match the paragraphs (1–4) with the pictures (A–D). Then choose a title for each paragraph.

Office Favorite   An Extraordinary Person
Family Life   Life and Death

 TRACK 2.26   **Now listen and check.**

3 LISTENING

 TRACK 2.27   **Carrie talks about her favorite TV series. Listen and choose the correct answer.**

1 What's the name of Carrie's favorite TV series?
   A *Changing Times.*
   B *Changing Places.*
2 What's it about?
   A People in a big city.
   B People in a small town.
3 Where does it take place?
   A In Santa Lucia.
   B In San Lorenzo.
4 How often is it on?
   A Every day.
   B Five times a week.
5 What was the most exciting episode?
   A Two people escaped from a fire.
   B Two people escaped from prison.
6 And what's happening right now?
   A They're looking for a mother.
   B They're looking for a murderer.

4 SPEAKING

Look at the questions in exercise 3. Ask another student about their favorite TV series.

What's your favorite TV series?

5 WRITING

Write a paragraph about a popular TV series. Use the text in this lesson to help you.

● What's the TV series about?
● Where does it take place?
● What happened in a recent episode?
● What's happening right now?
● What do you think will happen next?

LEARNER INDEPENDENCE

A

It's important to know which words can go together. Match the verbs with as many adverbs as possible.

Verbs
eat   drink   listen   look   speak
understand   walk   write

Adverbs
angrily   carefully   easily   happily
hungrily   quickly   slowly   thirstily

When you find useful word combinations, write them in your vocabulary notebook.

Verb + Adverb   *Verb + Noun*
eat hungrily   *take place*

B

To use a dictionary properly, you need to know the meanings of grammar words. Match these words with the grammar words in the Word Bank.

at   boring   camera   dancing
make   slowly   they   to see

Word Bank: GRAMMAR WORDS

adjective   adverb   gerund   infinitive
noun   preposition   pronoun   verb

Look at the Grammar pages at the end of each unit and find the grammar words.

C

PHRASEBOOK

 TRACK 2.28   **Find these useful expressions in Unit 4. Then listen and repeat.**

The big question is …
I have some bad news.
Oh, that's too bad!
I don't understand.
It doesn't make sense.
That's crazy!

Now write a four-line dialogue using two or more of the expressions.

A   I have some bad news.
B   What?
A   I can't get tickets for the concert.
B   Oh, that's too bad!

PROJECT

TV SHOWS

1 Work in a group and do a survey of your favorite TV shows. Make a list of the ten most popular shows in the group.

2 Look again at Unit 4 Lesson 4 and at the work you did in exercise 5 about a popular TV series. Then look at your group's list of most popular TV shows and choose three to write about.

3 Make notes about each show:

- What kind of show is it?
- Who is in it?   What channel is it on? When is it on?
- How often is it on?   Who do you watch it with?
- Why do you like it? Do you know a surprising fact about it?

4 Work together and write about the shows. Read your work carefully and correct any mistakes. Find photographs for each show from magazines or online. Show your work to the other groups.

Dancing with the Stars is a popular TV talent show in the U.S. In the show, celebrities have a week to learn and perform a new dance. It's on twice a week, on Monday and Tuesday evenings. All the family watch it and enjoy seeing the celebrities and their professional dance partners. A surprising fact about the show is that it appeals to people of all ages, from five to ninety.

GAME

WORD SQUARE

- Work in pairs.
- Write down as many English words as possible, using the letters in the square. You can go in any direction, but all the letters must touch. So, for example, you can make PLAY, but you can't make PART. And you can only use each letter once in any word.
- The pair that finds the most (correct!) words is the winner.

S	T	C	E
O	A	Y	A
R	P	L	R
O	E	N	I

CONSOLIDATION

1 **Write five sentences beginning *When I ...* using these phrases.**

get hungry   feel tired   feel thirsty
am bored   am by myself

When I get hungry, I have something to eat.

2 **Look at exercise 5 on page 59. Write sentences saying what will and won't happen in each situation.**

Emma won't say no. She'll say it's a great idea.

3 **Write a sentence using each adverb from the Word Bank on page 61, exercise 5.**

He shouted angrily at the boy who hit him.

4 **Look at the questions on page 63, exercise 5. Write a conversation between yourself and a friend.**

Me: What's your favorite TV series?

EXTENSION

1 **Work with another student and look again at the corrected statements in exercise 6 on page 57. Then role-play the conversation between Emma and Carrie, using the statements to help you.**

2 **Write sentences about your next birthday.**
- How old will you be?
- What will you do to celebrate?
- What gifts will you get?
- What do you think and hope will happen?

3 **Write about three movies which you enjoyed.**
- What are they called?
- Who is in them?
- What are they about?
- Why did you like them?

4 **Make a word map for television.**

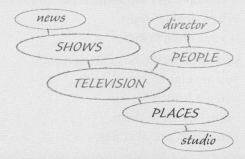

YOUR CHOICE!

HALF-MINUTE TALKS

- Work in a small group. Choose a letter of the alphabet (e.g., *T*). Each student says an "interesting" noun (singular or plural) beginning with that letter (e.g., *television, trees, teenagers*). Make a list of the nouns.
- One student chooses a noun from the list and talks for half a minute on that topic. The rest of the group can ask questions if the speaker can't think of anything more to say.
- Then choose another letter and speaker.

SAYING WORDS IN TWO WAYS

- Work in a small group. Make a list of five English words which you like, and think about why you like them. Is it their sound, or appearance, or meaning?
- Show your list to the group and say why you like the words.
- In turn, ask the rest of the group to say the words on their list in one of these pairs of ways:

quickly/slowly   loudly/quietly   happily/sadly
politely/rudely

*Hanna, say the words on your list
first quickly, then slowly.*

Grammar

OPEN CONDITIONAL WITH *IF/WHEN*

UNIT 4 LESSON 1

● We use the open conditional to talk about general truths, and cause and effect:
  If we mix red and green, we get yellow.
  If you don't like the pictures, you can delete them.
  When you look at digital photos, you see color pictures.

● In open conditional sentences, both verbs are in the simple present tense.

● The *if/when* clause may come after the main clause:
  What happens if we mix the three primary colors?
  When you take a picture, the computer compares …

PRACTICE: OPEN CONDITIONAL WITH *IF/WHEN*

1 **Match the beginnings with the endings.**
  1 If you mix blue, yellow, and light green,
  2 When I go to bed late,
  3 If you take five from thirteen,
  4 When people shout,
  5 If your phone rings,

  a you can check who's calling you.
  b you get eight.
  c you get brown.
  d I don't listen to them.
  e I feel tired the next day.

2 **Cross out *if* or *when* in one of the parts of each sentence.**
  1 When I'm happy, ~~when~~ everybody notices it.
  2 If you get into trouble, if you can call the police.
  3 If you take some medicine, if you feel better.
  4 When you get white, when you mix the primary colors of light.
  5 When your phone rings, when I always laugh.
  6 If we go for a run in the morning if the weather is good.

SIMPLE FUTURE: *WILL/WON'T*

UNIT 4 LESSON 2

● We can use *will* and *won't* (*will not*) to say what we predict or hope about the future:
  MP3 players will soon replace CDs.
  We won't know the answer for a few years.
  What will replace MP3 players?
  Which will we choose?

● We often use the simple future after these verbs and phrases:
  believe   be sure   expect   hope
  know   suppose   think

● *will* is a modal auxiliary verb:
  —it does not change with *he/she/it*.
  —we use *will* + infinitive without *to*:
  I think she will ~~to~~ say it's a great idea.

PRACTICE: SIMPLE FUTURE: *WILL/WON'T*

3 **Complete with *will* or *won't*.**
  1 What do you think _____ happen?
  2 I don't think Jay _____ say he's afraid of dogs.
  3 I'm sure Emma _____ miss a chance to go shopping.
  4 Lara _____ wear the black T-shirt because she loves black.
  5 It's raining, so they _____ have a picnic in the park.
  6 They _____ go to an expensive restaurant because they don't have a lot of money.

4 **Choose the correct words to complete the sentences.**
  1 Laptops will _____ lighter and lighter.
    A to get   **B** get   **C** gets   **D** got
  2 Communication _____ be easier in the future.
    A to   **B** do   **C** is   **D** will
  3 People won't _____ CDs anymore.
    A to buy   **B** buy   **C** buying   **D** buys
  4 Will you _____ the book today?
    A to finish   **B** finishes   **C** finishing   **D** finish

ADVERBS OF MANNER

Regular		Irregular	
Adjective	**Adverb**	**Adjective**	**Adverb**
bad	bad**ly**	early	early
normal	normal**ly**	fast	fast
proper	proper**ly**	good	well
quick	quick**ly**	hard	hard
angry	angr**ily**	late	late
happy	happ**ily**		

● We use adverbs of manner to describe **how** we do something.
  You spoke too fast.
  Actors work extremely hard.

● **Spelling**:

Most adjectives add *ly*:
  *normal—normal**ly**   proper—proper**ly***

Adjectives ending in *y* change the *y* to *i* and add *ly*:
  *happy—happ**ily**   angry—angr**ily***

Adjectives ending in *ble* drop the *e* and add *y*:
  *comforta**ble**—comforta**bly**   terri**ble**—terri**bly***

PRACTICE: ADVERBS OF MANNER

5 **Complete with adverbs of manner. You can look back at page 60.**
1 Steve thought that the group acted very _____.
2 They spoke _____, but the director thought they spoke too _____.
3 There wasn't time for them to rehearse _____.
4 The director thought the group acted _____.
5 Actors work _____ doing drama exercises.

6 **Complete with adverbs of manner which are true for you.**
1 I sing _____.
2 I act _____.
3 I run _____.
4 I study _____.
5 I speak _____.

Review UNIT 3 & UNIT 4

1 Read and choose the best words.

HOLLYWOOD HERE I COME!

Is there life after soaps? TV star Angie Gold thinks so. She is leaving New York for a new career in Hollywood. When I met her in her Manhattan apartment, she (1) got/was getting ready for the trip to California.

"Everything is working out (2) beautiful/ beautifully," Angie said. "I (3) finished/was finishing filming here last week, and I start work in Hollywood next month. But I'm going to take a vacation first!"

She is going to play the part of a pop star in a movie. "I almost (4) didn't accept/wasn't accepting the part (5) so/because there's a lot of singing in the movie." Angie explained. "Everyone says that I sing pretty (6) good/well, but I'm (7) nervous/ nervously about it. I know that things won't be easy there at first, but I enjoy working (8) hard/ hardly. You can do anything if you (9) want/ wanted it (10) bad/badly enough."

Good luck, Angie!

2 Complete with the simple past of these verbs.

be destroy die go live
marry take work write

1 Shakespeare _____ Anne Hathaway in 1582.
2 When Shakespeare _____ in 1616, he _____ exactly 52 years old.
3 Charles Dickens _____ in Portsmouth until 1823.
4 He _____ in a factory at the age of 12.
5 He _____ 14 very successful novels.
6 The San Francisco earthquake _____ most of the city.
7 Arnold Genthe _____ pictures of the fire.
8 People _____ to watch the fire.

3 Ask and answer.
Alex/visit the museum ✗/go to a music store ✔

Did Alex visit the museum? **No, he didn't.**

Did he go to a music store? **Yes, he did.**

1 Jay/take a cable car ✔/walk up the hill ✗
2 Ramón and Silvana/visit a theater ✗/see an exhibit ✔
3 Lara/lose her camera ✗/take lots of pictures ✔
4 the group/have a picnic ✔/go to a restaurant ✗
5 Emma/visit the temple ✗/wait outside ✔

Now write sentences using the simple past.
Alex didn't visit the museum. He went to a music store.

4 Complete with the correct preposition of time.

1 _____ July
2 _____ Monday
3 _____ 5:30
4 _____ 2010
5 _____ the evening
6 _____ Friday afternoon
7 _____ midnight
8 _____ May 5
9 _____ the winter

5 Write sentences using the past progressive + *when* + simple past.
Ryan/sail/fall overboard
Ryan was sailing when he fell overboard.

1 Alex/take pictures/he/drop his bag
2 Lara/do gymnastics/she/hurt her foot
3 Jay and Emma/dance/see Steve
4 Carrie/record an interview/the phone/ring
5 Ramón/listen to music/he/fall asleep

6 Write sentences using the simple past + *because* + past progressive.
Carrie/go home early/she/not feel well
Carrie went home early because she wasn't feeling well.

1 Steve/stay in the hotel/he/take care of the group
2 Emma/get lost/she/not think
3 Jay and Lara/not play tennis/it/rain
4 Ramón/have a hot shower/he/feel cold
5 Silvana/not dance/her feet/hurt

7 Match the beginnings with the endings.

1 When you send someone a text message,
2 If you press the red button,
3 When you add two and two,
4 If you mix red and green light,
5 When I open the door,

a it makes a funny noise.
b you get yellow.
c their cell phone beeps.
d the TV comes on.
e you get four.

68

8 Complete this phone conversation with *will* or *won't*.

ANGIE I hope nothing __1__ go wrong when I'm in Hollywood.

NICK Don't worry. You __2__ have a great time, you know that. And I promise I __3__ e-mail you as often as I can.

ANGIE I hope you __4__ forget me.

NICK Of course I __5__. I __6__ call you once a week.

ANGIE Once a week! Why __7__ you call every day? You know how much I __8__ miss you.

NICK Because of the three-hour time difference between New York and California. You __9__ want to talk to me in the middle of the night!

ANGIE __10__ you think about me every day?

NICK Of course I __11__. But I think you __12__ be too busy to think about me!

9 Complete with the correct adverb of manner.

early easy good happy late
nervous polite quiet slow

1 Sh! Please talk _____.

2 The bus left _____ and they missed it.

3 Everyone enjoyed the drama exercises and smiled _____.

4 Lara danced _____ and everyone watched her.

5 Silvana was worried about pickpockets and looked around _____.

6 "Excuse me, can you help me, please?" Ramón asked _____.

7 You feel tired when you go to bed _____.

8 Please say that again _____.

9 I can do this exercise _____!

VOCABULARY

10 Complete with six of these words.

atmosphere bestseller building career
documentary harbor primary tragedy

1 Last night we watched a TV _____ about meteorites.

2 Red and blue are _____ colors.

3 *Hamlet* is a famous _____ by Shakespeare.

4 Grace Cathedral is a beautiful _____.

5 It's hard to make a successful _____ as an actor.

6 It's a very popular novel—it's a _____.

11 Match the verbs in list A with the words and phrases in list B.

	A	B
1	fall	a button
2	have	a play
3	make	hard
4	press	place
5	rehearse	sense
6	take	a story
7	tell	fun
8	work	overboard

LEARNER INDEPENDENCE

SELF ASSESSMENT

Look back at Lessons 1–3 in Units 3 and 4

How good are you at …?	✔ Fine	? Not sure
1 Talking about past events *1 Walt Disney made the first cartoon movie with sound in 1928.* pp98–99 exercises 1–5, and pp100–101 exercises 2–4	☐	☐
2 Describing what was happening pp102–103 exercises 2–4	☐	☐
3 Asking for and giving reasons p103 exercise 5	☐	☐
4 Talking about cause and effect pp110–111 exercises 1–3	☐	☐
5 Making predictions pp112–113 exercises 2 and 3	☐	☐
6 Talking about the way people do things p114 exercises 1–3	☐	☐

Not sure? Take a look at Grammar pages 52–53 and 66–67, and do the Workbook exercise(s) again.

Now write an example for 1–6.

Congratulations!

It's the end of *Insights 3*. Now look at your progress.

Let's start with grammar and vocabulary.

GRAMMAR

Look through the Grammar pages at the end of each unit, and see what you learned in *Insights 3*.

VOCABULARY

The Word List on page 122 lists all the new words in *Insights 3*, as well as groups of words by topic. Choose some topics (e.g., Jobs, Town Facilities), and write a list of all the words you can remember for each one.

But you learned more than grammar and vocabulary. In *Insights 3*, you also learned to communicate.

COMMUNICATION

You can ...

Describe where people are and what they are doing

Ask and answer questions about people's jobs

Talk about carnivals and festivals

Say what people should and shouldn't do in your country

Interview people about what they love/hate doing

Interview people about what they did last weekend

Talk about the life of a famous person

Say what you think will happen next

Describe your favorite TV show

What else can you do?

LISTENING

You can listen to and understand …

An interview about likes and dislikes

A description of a celebration

A conversation about recent activities

A story of an accident

A description of the life of a famous person

Drama exercises

What else can you listen to and understand?

You also have another very important skill.

LEARNER INDEPENDENCE

You learned …

Ways of finding the meanings of words

How to keep a personal phrasebook

Ways of learning words

How to assess your own progress

How to learn words through association

How to group and remember words by topic

How words can make combinations

Words we use to describe grammar

HOW DO YOU FEEL?

Have a class discussion about your English classes and *Insights 3*.

Talk about

- Three things you like about the classes and the book.
- Activities and exercises you would like to do more or less often.
- Something you would like to change.
- Something you would like to do in your English classes next year.

Now write a note to your teacher giving your opinions.

You also have other language skills.

WRITING

You can write …

A description of a photo

A personal profile

A description of a place in your country

A diary entry

A description of the life of a famous person

Information about the history of your town

Predictions about the future

A description of a TV show

What else can you write?

READING

You can read …

Information about a social networking site

An article with personal information

A sightseeing guide

An article about carnivals

A description of a festival

A questionnaire

An article about a historical event

A biography of a famous person

An article about the history of a city

A magazine article about TV shows

What else can you read?

End of the Student's Book section

Judy Garton-Sprenger and Philip Prowse
with Marcelo Baccarin, Helena Gomm,
and Catherine Smith

WORKBOOK

MACMILLAN

1 DO YOU REALLY SPEAK CHINESE?

1 **READING**

Read the dialogue. Then put a check (✔) in the chart for the things that Alex and Lara like and a cross (✗) for the things they don't like.

ALEX   Oh, look at those dogs! I love dogs!

LARA   Do you? I don't like them at all.

ALEX   So what things do you like? How about basketball?

LARA   No, I never play basketball, but I like swimming.

ALEX   I love basketball. I play it on the weekend. I do karate too, but I don't like swimming. What about music? I love music. Do you like it?

LARA   Yes, I love rock music. I go to a music club every Saturday, after the movies.

ALEX   Oh, I go to the movies on Saturdays too! I love the movies.

LARA   Then let's go together next Saturday!

	dogs	basketball	swimming	music	the movies
Alex	✔				
Lara	✗				

2 **SIMPLE PRESENT AFFIRMATIVE**

Complete with the simple present of these verbs.

come   do   drink   ~~go~~   like   play

1 Lara ___goes___ to the movies on Saturdays.

2 She _____ from Recife.

3 Lara and Alex _____ rock music.

4 Alex _____ basketball on the weekend.

5 He also _____ karate on the weekend.

6 We _____ coffee for breakfast.

3 **SIMPLE PRESENT AFFIRMATIVE AND NEGATIVE**

Write sentences.

1 Jay/come/from Australia ✗

   Jay doesn't come from Australia.
   from the U.S. ✔
   He comes from the U.S.

2 Emma/speak/Italian ✔

   _____

   Chinese ✗

   _____

3 Lara and Alex/go/to the movies on Saturdays ✔

   _____

   to the theater ✗

   _____

4 Alex/play/basketball ✔

   _____

   soccer ✗

   _____

5 Jay and Alex/like/dogs ✔

   _____

   cats ✗

   _____

6 I/come/from San Francisco ✗

   _____

   from ... ✔

   _____

4 SIMPLE PRESENT QUESTIONS AND SHORT ANSWERS

Complete Carrie's questions. Then write the answers. Who is A?

CARRIE **(1)** _Do you speak_ (speak) French?

A **(2)** Yes, _____.

CARRIE **(3)** _____ (come) from Vancouver?

A **(4)** No, _____.

CARRIE **(5)** _____ (like) horses?

A **(6)** Yes, _____.

CARRIE **(7)** _____ (do) yoga?

A **(8)** Yes, _____.

5 VOCABULARY

Complete the word maps with these words.

soccer   DVDs   yoga   to bed   ~~swimming~~
karate   movies   gymnastics   TV   basketball
to the movies   computer games

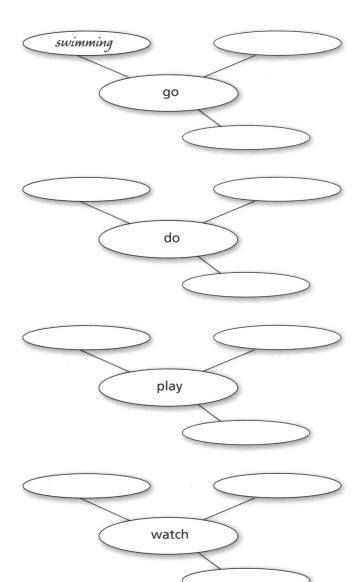

6 PRONUNCIATION

Do they rhyme (✔) or not (✗)?

1	how	know	✗
2	see	tea	
3	speak	week	
4	come	from	
5	do	go	
6	what	not	
7	watch	much	
8	you	too	

7 VOCABULARY

Read the text and cross out eight more extra words.

Here are some facts ~~what~~ about our World2day contest winners. Emma from Vancouver has speaks English, Italian, and fifty French. Silvana chats with her keys friends online every evening in English and but Spanish! Ramón really likes music and he never loves hip-hop and rap! Lara does opens gymnastics every Friday afternoon and then she goes swimming in a the evening door.

Now write the extra words. Can you answer the question they make?

Q _What_ _____

_____

A _____

➡ EXTENSION

Imagine you are one of the World2day contest winners. Write three sentences about yourself.

UNIT 1

MAKING FRIENDS

2 YOU'RE STANDING ON MY FOOT!

Every year, 16 million people visit San Francisco, and many of them go to the area of Fisherman's Wharf. It's the most popular tourist attraction in the city. A lot of the visitors like to ride on the San Francisco carousel. It has two levels and 1,800 lights. There are 32 animals to ride on, including sea lions, pandas, and horses. Each ride costs $3.00 and takes around four minutes. Near the carousel is the Aquarium of the Bay, where you can see 20,000 sea animals. The aquarium is very popular and has 600,000 visitors every year.

1 READING

Read about Fisherman's Wharf in San Francisco. Match the numbers in list A with the things in list B.

A		B	
a	3	1	the number of visitors to the city per year
b	20,000	2	the number of levels on the carousel
c	1,800	3	the number of visitors to the aquarium per year
d	16 million	4	the number of lights on the carousel
e	32	5	the number of animals in the aquarium
f	600,000	6	the number of dollars a ride costs
g	2	7	the number of animals on the carousel

2 PRESENT PROGRESSIVE AFFIRMATIVE

Look at the photo on the right (also on pages 10 and 11). Then complete with the present progressive of these verbs.

take ~~hold~~ stand tell listen wear watch help

1 Alex _____is holding_____ a camera.
2 Steve _____ a black jacket.
3 Steve _____ everyone about San Francisco.
4 Lara _____ next to Steve.
5 Silvana _____ Alex with his camera.
6 Jay and Lara _____ to Steve.
7 The thin man_____ the girl's wallet.
8 The girl _____ the juggler.

3 RELATIVE PRONOUNS

Rewrite sentences 1–6 in exercise 2 using *who* or *that*.

1 _Alex is the boy who/that is holding a camera._
2 _____
   _____
3 _____
   _____
4 _____
   _____
5 _____
   _____
6 _____
   _____

4 PRESENT PROGRESSIVE AFFIRMATIVE AND NEGATIVE

Write sentences about the people in the photo.

1 Jay/hold a bag/hold an umbrella
   Jay isn't holding a bag.
   He's holding an umbrella.
2 Ramón/sit next to Emma/stand next to Emma
   _____
   _____
3 Lara/read a magazine/look at the map
   _____
   _____
4 The girl/listen to Steve/watch the juggler
   _____
   _____
5 Alex and Silvana/take pictures/check the camera
   _____
   _____

PRESENT PROGRESSIVE QUESTIONS

Write questions and answers about the people in the photo.

1 Jay/look at the thin man   (listen to Steve)

Is Jay looking at the thin man?   *No, he isn't. He's listening to Steve.*

2 Lara/make a phone call   (look at the map)

_____   _____

3 Steve/wear a hat   (wear a jacket)

_____   _____

4 the girl/take pictures   (watch the juggler)

_____   _____

5 Alex and Silvana/hold hands   (check the camera)

_____   _____

6 Steve/tell a joke   (talk about San Francisco)

_____   _____

6 **VOCABULARY**

Find nine words for things you wear in the word square. Then label the pictures.

T	P	A	N	T	S	H	S
O	S	Q	I	R	T	A	H
P	J	E	A	N	S	T	I
S	W	E	A	T	E	R	R
H	M	J	A	C	K	E	T
O	D	I	L	Y	U	C	W
E	X	F	S	Q	O	E	N
S	N	E	A	K	E	R	S

1   *sweater*   **2** _____

3 _____   **4** _____

5 _____   **6** _____   **7** _____   **8** _____   **9** _____

7 **PRONUNCIATION**

Find the rhyming words.

feel foot hand knows play make dress ~~wide~~

1 guide _wide_   **5** take _____

2 put _____   **6** those _____

3 stand _____   **7** way _____

4 wheel _____   **8** guess _____

EXTENSION

Write two sentences saying what you are wearing today. Write another sentence saying what a friend is wearing.

UNIT 1

3 IT'S MY SISTER'S BIRTHDAY

1 READING

Read the tweets on the right and answer these questions.

1 What is Teri doing now?

_____

2 Is Val drinking a soda?

_____

3 What is Anthony doing?

_____

4 What's Mark's problem?

_____

5 What is Clark's problem?

_____

 AlbTerrrri Teri Albretch
Celebrating sister's birthday! Luv u Bella!
2 minutes ago

 ToyToyToy Val Toy
I'm having a meal at this great place.
Check it out! **http://ow.li/7o3CG**
31 minutes ago

 onemorebaker Anthony Baker
Guess who's sitting next to me on the plane
to LA? **twitpic.com/85jf4t**
54 minutes ago

 AlbBel99 Isabella Albretch
Thank you so much everyone!
1 hour ago

 quietbrig Mark Brigger
Camera on my cell phone not working!!!! ☹
Sorry guys! No pictures!
1 hour ago

BballPitchNathe Clark Nathe
Rain! Rain! Rain! I guess this means no pool
or park today! We're off to see a movie.
2 hours ago

2 WHOSE ...? AND POSSESSIVE 'S

Follow the paths. Then write questions and answers.

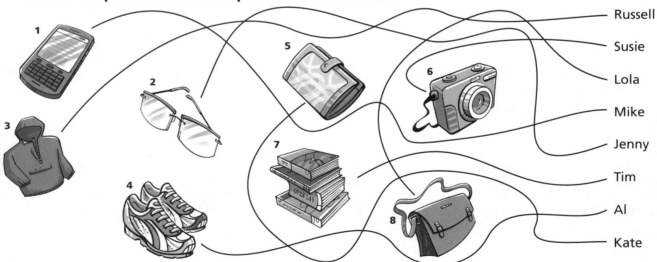

Russell
Susie
Lola
Mike
Jenny
Tim
Al
Kate

1 *Whose cell phone is this?* _____ *It's Mike's cell phone.* _____
2 *Whose glasses are these?* _____ *They're Jenny's glasses.* _____
3 _____ _____
4 _____ _____
5 _____ _____
6 _____ _____
7 _____ _____
8 _____ _____

3 WHOSE OR WHO'S

Complete with *Whose* or *Who's*.

1 ___*Who's*___ the man in the jacket?
2 _____ dog is this?
3 _____ the girl on the right?
4 _____ talking to Bill?
5 _____ are these magazines?
6 _____ favorite band is Linkin Park?

4 POSSESSIVE 'S OR IS

What does *'s* mean in these sentences?

1 What's that man doing?   possession ☐   is ☑
2 Is this Anna's guitar?   possession ☐   is ☐
3 Luke's reading a play.   possession ☐   is ☐
4 Rosie's a reporter.   possession ☐   is ☐
5 It's a play about nurses.   possession ☐   is ☐
6 Bill's job is interesting.   possession ☐   is ☐

5 POSSESSIVE ADJECTIVES AND PRONOUNS

Read. Then write sentences using possessive adjectives and possessive pronouns.

1 She has a guitar.
   ___*It's her guitar. It's hers.*___
2 We have some flowers.
   ___*They're*___
3 You have a camera.
   _____
4 She has some DVDs.
   _____
5 I have a dog.
   _____
6 They have some magazines.
   _____
7 He has some books.
   _____
8 They have a car.
   _____

6 SIMPLE PRESENT AND PRESENT PROGRESSIVE

Choose the correct words to complete the sentences.

1 Rosie can't speak to you now. She …
   Linkin Park.
   A interviews   **B** 's interviewing
2 Bill often … on the weekend.
   A works   **B** 's working
3 Anna … songs every day.
   A writes   **B** 's writing
4 Look at Scott! He … with Goldie.
   A plays   **B** 's playing
5 Teri and her sister are in a restaurant.
   They … a meal.
   A have   **B** 're having
6 She's a musician. She … the guitar
   and sings.
   A plays   **B** 's playing
7 We … gymnastics classes every Saturday.
   A have   **B** 're having
8 Where …? Can I come with you?
   A do you go   **B** are you going
9 Luke … up late.
   A never gets   **B** 's never getting
10 Scott and Bill … to New York right now.
   A don't fly   **B** aren't flying

7 VOCABULARY

Match the beginnings of the words with the endings to make jobs. Then write the words.

1 rep	fighter	1	*reporter*
2 pil	ist	2	_____
3 fire	or	3	_____
4 photo	cher	4	_____
5 music	orter	5	_____
6 reception	ian	6	_____
7 act	ot	7	_____
8 tea	grapher	8	_____

> ### EXTENSION
> **Write sentences about three members of your family. Say what they do and what you think they're doing right now.**

UNIT 1

 4 PERSONAL PROFILES
● Integrated Skills

1 READING

Carrie interviews Alex for the World2day website.
Match his answers with the questions.

FIVE MINUTES WITH...
ALEX

WORLD2DAY

Alex is one of the winners of the World2day vacation contest. What's he like? Find out here!

Carrie's questions:

1 Where do you live?   j
2 What are your favorite clothes?
3 What are your favorite colors?
4 What is your favorite word?
5 What makes you angry?
6 What makes you happy?
7 What languages do you speak?
8 Is there someone very important to you?
9 Is there something special you do every day?
10 What are you reading right now?

Alex's answers:

a   "Peanut butter." I eat it on toast for breakfast!
b   When my team wins at basketball!
c   Red and blue.
d   I try to write in my journal every day.
e   English, of course!
f   My blue T-shirt and black jeans.
g   *The Lord of the Rings.* The movie was amazing, so I wanted to read the book.
h   When I play chess with my sister and she wins!
i   My grandmother is a very special person for me.
j   In Sydney, near the ocean.

2 WRITING

Complete this profile of Alex for World2day. You can use the profile of Jay on page 15 to help you.

Alex

Alex is our winner from Australia and he lives in Sydney, near the ocean. His favorite clothes
_____
_____
_____
_____

3 CROSSWORD

Complete the crossword puzzle.

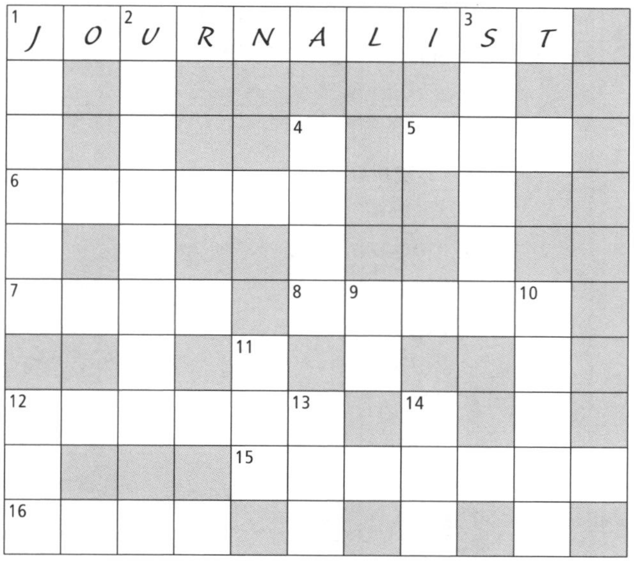

J	O	U	R	N	A	L	I	S	T	

(Crossword grid with answer 1 ACROSS filled in as JOURNALIST)

ACROSS →

1 This is Carrie's job. (10)
5 A hot drink. (3)
6 A sport in which you fight with your hands and feet. (6)
7 Someone who isn't short is … (4)
8 Alex likes peanut butter on his … (5)
12 Fisherman's Wharf and Union Square are … in San Francisco. (6)
15 Someone who works in a school. (7)
16 Opposite of *false*. (4)

DOWN ↓

1 A short coat. (6)
2 Hold this over your head when it rains. (8)
3 Silvana … three languages. (6)
4 You can send a … message from a cell phone. (4)
9 Silvana goes to the movies … Saturdays. (2)
10 A photographer is someone who … pictures. (5)
11 A doctor for animals. (3)
12 Dogs and cats are types of this. (3)
13 What's happening? I can't … a thing. (3)
14 Perform in a movie or play. (3)

LEARNER INDEPENDENCE

YOUR PERSONAL PHRASEBOOK

Read the definitions and complete the examples.

1 *When you do this, you think about someone and want to be with them.*
I often _____ my friends when I'm on vacation.

2 *People keep their money in this.*
Put your _____ somewhere safe—you don't want a pickpocket to take it.

3 *This is a place where you can walk, or play soccer, for example.*
Jay plays with his dog in the
_____.

4 *This is something you carry when it rains.*
I always take my _____ when I go to Seattle.

5 *This is someone who plays an instrument.*
I like that _____'s songs.
Let's buy her CD.

When you write new words and expressions in your personal phrasebook, it's useful to write an example sentence to show their meaning.

UNIT 1 MAKING FRIENDS

Insights EXTRA!

CONSOLIDATION

Welcome!

Complete with *I, he, she, we,* or *they*.

CARRIE (**1**) _____ 'm Carrie and this is Ramón.
(**2**) _____ 's from Mexico. Emma is from Vancouver.
(**3**) _____ 's Canadian. Lara is Brazilian and (**4**) _____ 's
from Recife. Alex is Australian and (**5**) _____ 's from
Sydney. This is Silvana and (**6**) _____ 's Argentine. Jay is
from the U.S. (**7**) _____ 's American. (**8**) _____ 're all
winners of the World2day contest. Today, (**9**) _____ 're
all in San Francisco.

1 **Complete with the simple present of these verbs.**

come   go   not like   not live   play   speak   teach   watch

1 Emma's mother _____ yoga.

2 Emma _____ sea lions.

3 Jay never _____ computer games.

4 Do you _____ DVDs?

5 Silvana and Emma both _____ French.

6 Lara _____ swimming on Fridays.

7 Emma _____ from Canada.

8 I _____ in Miami.

2 **Look again at the photo on pages 10 and 11. Write questions and short answers.**

1 Ramón/wear/an orange shirt
   Is Ramón wearing an orange shirt?
   No, he isn't.

2 Alex and Silvana/listen to Steve

   _____

   _____

3 Emma/wear/a green top

   _____

   _____

4 the girl in the orange top/smile

   _____

   _____

5 Ramón/stand/on Emma's foot

   _____

   _____

3 **Write questions with *Whose* and then answer them.**

1 dog _____ *Whose dog is this?* _____
   Scott _____ *It's Scott's.* _____

2 sneakers _____

   Jay _____

3 cell phone _____

   Teresa _____

4 magazines _____

   Luke _____

5 bag _____

   Bill _____

6 CDs _____

   Anna _____

4 **Put the words in the right order. Then answer the questions for you.**

1 clothes your are what favorite
   What are your favorite clothes?

   _____

2 makes happy you what

   _____

   _____

3 speak what do languages you

   _____

   _____

4 there you to is important someone very

   _____

   _____

5 reading now you right what are

   _____

   _____

SPELLING

Complete these words from Unit 1.

1 g y mn _a_ st _i_ cs   **5** m__s__ci__n

2 fav__rit__   **6** w__ll__t

3 sw____t__r   **7** imp__rt__nt

4 f__m__us   **8** lang__ag__

BRAINTEASER

What has a face and two hands, but no legs?

Answer on page 97.

Welcome!

Complete with these countries. One can be used twice.

Argentina   Australia   Brazil   Canada   Mexico   the U.S.

1 They speak English in _____,
_____, and _____.

2 They speak French in _____.

3 They speak Spanish in _____
and _____.

4 They speak Portuguese in _____.

1 Correct these sentences.

1 Alex ~~not~~ live in the U.S.
    does

2 He play soccer every week.

3 What languages you speak?

4 Jay don't believe Emma speaks Chinese.

5 Does she drinks tea for breakfast?

2 Complete with the simple present or present progressive of these verbs.

get   have   know   like   play   give

1 Jay and Lara _____ a good time in San Francisco.

2 Steve _____ them a tour of the city.

3 _____ you _____ what *joke* means?

4 Silvana _____ sea lions.

5 Listen! Alex _____ the guitar.

6 What time _____ you usually _____ up?

3 Look at the photo on pages 10 and 11. What do the words in bold refer to?

1 Lara looks at **it** when she's lost.
    her map
    _____

2 Emma uses **it** to carry important things.
    _____

3 Steve wears **it** to stay warm.
    _____

4 Alex uses **it** to take pictures.
    _____

5 Jay wears **them** on his feet.
    _____

4 Read this profile of Emma and cross out seven more extra words.

Emma

Emma is from the ~~what~~ beautiful city of Vancouver in Canada. She lives goes with her parents and her brother, Ryan. Her favorite clothes are to party dresses. Her favorite word is "independence" and her favorite color is bed red. People who tell her what to do with make her angry, and shopping its makes her happy. Her two shoes cats, Fred and Ginger, are very important to her, and something she does on every morning is check her e-mail.

Now write the extra words in your notebook. Can you answer the question they make?

WEB WATCH

Look up San Francisco on the Internet and find out more about tourist attractions in the city. Look up new words in the dictionary and make a *Sightseeing* section in your vocabulary notebook.

SPELLING

Read and complete with the correct form of these words.

country   do   finish   phone

Rule: Spelling of plural nouns and third person singular verbs

- We add *s* to most words to form plural nouns or third person singular verbs:
  *computer**s**   drink**s**   choose**s*** (1) _____

- We add *es* to words ending in *ch, sh, ss, x:*
  *watch**es*** (2) _____ *dress**es**   box**es***

- For words ending in consonant + *y*, we change *y* to *i* and add *es*:
  country → (3) _____
  party → *part**ies**   try* → *tr**ies***
  BUT boy → *boy**s**   play* → *play**s**   say* → *say**s***

- We add *s* to some nouns ending in *o* (*photo**s**, piano**s***), but we add *es* to other nouns and all verbs ending in *o*:
  *potato**es*** (4) _____ *go**es***

BRAINTEASER

A man and a woman are standing on the same piece of newspaper. But they can't touch each other. Why not?

Answer on page 97.

UNIT 1 Culture

WELCOME TO SAN FRANCISCO

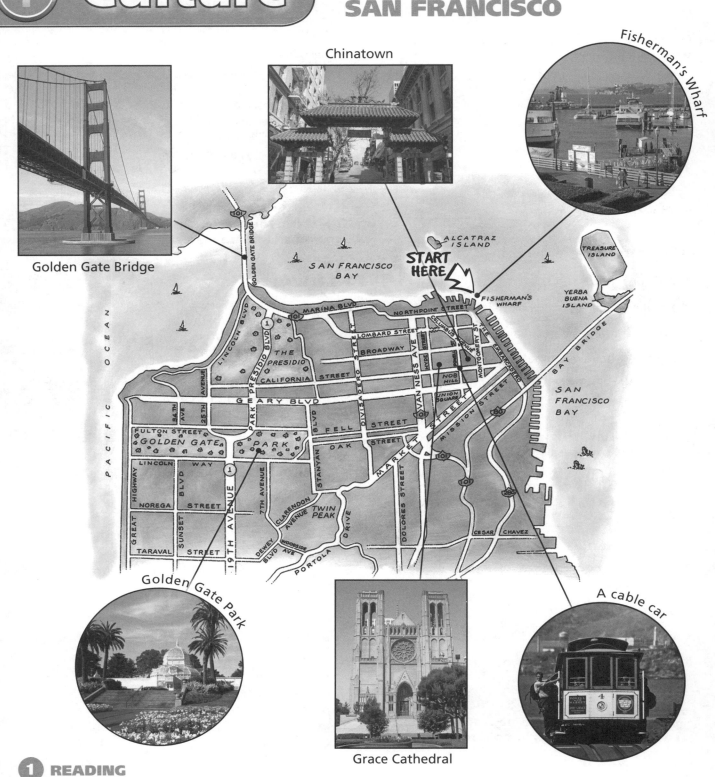

Chinatown

Fisherman's Wharf

Golden Gate Bridge

Golden Gate Park

A cable car

Grace Cathedral

1 READING

Look at the photos of places and things in San Francisco and match them with these descriptions.

1 There are temples, stores, and restaurants here. _____

2 You can take a boat ride from here. _____

3 This was the longest suspension bridge in the world when it opened. _____

4 This is a famous church. _____

5 This is one of the largest city parks in the world. _____

6 You can ride up the hills on this. _____

2 READING

The World2day group are on a bus sightseeing tour. Read and follow the route
of the bus on the map. Number the places in the order the bus passes them.

Welcome to the World2day San Francisco sightseeing
tour. You all have a map of the city, and here is the
route of our tour.

We're at Fisherman's Wharf—can you find that on your map? It's
on San Francisco Bay, where it says START HERE! First, we go along
the waterfront, and then we drive into Chinatown. From there, we
go up Nob Hill—it's the most famous hill in San Francisco and it
has great views over the city. We're going up by bus, but you can
also go up by cable car. We stop by Grace Cathedral at the top of
the hill and you can get out and take pictures. Then we get back
on the bus and go across town to Golden Gate Park. It's huge, over
four square kilometers, and it goes all the way to the Pacific Ocean.
It's beautiful and there's lots to do there. But I'm afraid there isn't
time to walk around the park today because next we're off to the
Golden Gate Bridge. We stop there so you can take pictures. Back
on the bus, we drive east along the bay, and finally we're back
where we started at Fisherman's Wharf.

3 VOCABULARY

Find five words for people and five words for
places in the word square. All the words are
on pages 18 and 19.

S	C	B	R	I	D	G	E	P	S	W	S
R	O	C	K	S	I	N	G	E	R	A	T
E	M	O	O	V	T	H	M	U	A	T	A
C	O	R	O	T	H	E	W	A	Q	E	S
A	V	E	E	V	E	T	A	R	U	R	T
Y	I	U	A	B	M	U	R	T	A	F	R
O	E	L	T	H	E	A	T	E	R	A	O
A	S	T	O	R	P	T	E	E	I	L	N
Y	T	S	R	T	A	E	R	S	U	L	A
R	A	T	O	U	R	I	S	T	M	E	U
T	R	P	I	C	K	P	O	C	K	E	T

Now write the words from the square in the
correct list.

People   **Places**

_____   _____

_____   _____

_____   _____

_____   _____

_____   _____

4 VOCABULARY

Match the words in list A with the words
in list B to make eight compound words.
Then write the words.

A		B		
1	cable	bridge	1	*cable car*
2	movie	attraction	2	_____
3	salt	park	3	_____
4	theme	show	4	_____
5	circus	trip	5	_____
6	suspension	star	6	_____
7	boat	car	7	_____
8	tourist	water	8	_____

CARNIVALS AROUND THE WORLD

There are carnivals all over the world in February or March each year. The biggest ones are in Rio de Janeiro, Trinidad, and New Orleans. But there are lots of other carnivals …

Cologne, Germany

The carnival lasts three days and the main events are in the old part of the city. The festival ends with an eight-kilometer parade and people wear special costumes to celebrate the history of their city.

Nice, France

This is a family-friendly festival, with contests for children in the parks and on the beach. There are daily parades, and people throw flowers to the crowd.

Red Lodge, Montana, USA

This is a celebration with a difference—it combines a traditional winter festival with a carnival. Lots of people arrive in costumes and have fun in the snow. There are snow sculptures, snowmobile races, and a parade on Saturday night.

Venice, Italy

This is a romantic carnival: people wear exotic 18th-century costumes and masks over their faces. For several days, there are people dancing in the squares, parties through the streets and along the canals, and fireworks over the city at night.

Sydney, Australia

About 750,000 people go to Sydney's one-day carnival parade, along with some of the best bands and DJs from around the world. After the main celebration, there are noisy parties in every bar, club, and swimming pool in Sydney!

1 READING

Read the text. Then read the sentences and write *T* (true) or *F* (false).

1 The Red Lodge festival is in the summer. ☐

2 There are parades at the Cologne, Nice, and Red Lodge carnivals. ☐

3 People wear costumes at three of the carnivals. ☐

4 The best carnival for children is in Nice. ☐

5 You can go to carnival parties in Venice and Sydney. ☐

6 You can't dance at the Venice carnival. ☐

2 VOCABULARY

Match the adjectives in list A with their opposites in list B.

A	B
1 old	a dangerous
2 hot	b quiet
3 wet	c expensive
4 noisy	d dry
5 safe	e cold
6 cheap	f modern

3 COMPARATIVE ADJECTIVES

Complete with comparative adjectives.

1 The Venice carnival lasts _longer_____ than the Sydney carnival. (long)

2 The Sydney carnival has _____ music than the Montana carnival. (good)

3 The Venice carnival is _____ than the Red Lodge carnival. (popular)

4 The weather is _____ in Red Lodge than in Nice. (cold)

5 The Sydney carnival is _____ than the Venice carnival. (noisy)

6 The Venice carnival is _____ than the Sydney carnival. (exotic)

4 COMPARATIVE AND SUPERLATIVE ADJECTIVES

Complete the chart.

Adjective	Comparative	Superlative
colorful	more colorful	the most colorful
dangerous		
dry		
expensive		
hungry		
nice		
old		
popular		
spectacular		
warm		
wet		

5 COMPARATIVE ADJECTIVES

Write sentences.

1 Brazil/Australia (large)

_Brazil is larger than Australia._____

2 Sydney/Vancouver (warm)

_____

3 Emma/Lara (noisy)

_____

4 taxis/buses (expensive)

_____

5 driving/flying (dangerous)

_____

6 Steve/Jay (old)

_____

6 COMPARATIVE AND SUPERLATIVE ADJECTIVES

Write phrases that mean the same, using _less_ or _the least_ and these adjectives.

difficult   expensive   ~~modern~~   noisy
safe   tall   usual   ~~warm~~

1 colder _____ _less warm_____
2 the most traditional __ _the least modern_____
3 the cheapest _____
4 the quietest _____
5 more unusual _____
6 shorter _____
7 the easiest _____
8 more dangerous _____

7 PRONUNCIATION

Mark the stressed syllable.

■
carnival   famous   giant   million

parade   region   stadium

> **EXTENSION**
> **Look at the chart and write sentences about the three cities in your notebook.**

City	Chicago	Rio	Rome
Age	175 years old	450 years old	2,750 years old
Population	3 million	6 million	2.7 million
Winter	January -6°C	July 25°C	January 10°C
Summer	July 23°C	January 31°C	July 30°C

Rio is older than Chicago, but Rome is the oldest city.

UNIT 2 FESTIVALS

2 WE SHOULD STAY TOGETHER

1 READING

Read the tips for tourists in San Francisco. Match the tips with the sentences below.

Tips for tourists in San Francisco

1. You should get a good map of the city.
2. You should cover your guidebook so you don't look like a tourist.
3. You shouldn't go out without a sunhat.
4. You should buy a Muni Passport travel card to use on buses and cable cars.
5. You shouldn't get on a bus without a ticket.
6. You shouldn't put your money in the back pocket of your jeans.
7. You shouldn't carry a lot of money with you.
8. You should leave your passport at your hotel.

a This tip will make traveling around the city cheaper. _4_

b These four tips are about safety. _____, _____, _____, _____

c This tip is about the weather. _____

d This tip is about finding your way around. _____

e This tip tells you not to do something which is against the law. _____

f These two tips are about something you should buy. _____, _____

2 SHOULD AND SHOULDN'T

The World2day group have some problems. Give them advice using these phrases.

You should ...	You shouldn't ...
get up for breakfast	take it out of the hotel
~~wear more comfortable shoes~~	go by yourself
buy an umbrella	~~walk so far~~
leave it at the reception desk	stay out in the rain
listen to him	stay in bed

1 _You should wear more comfortable shoes._
  You shouldn't walk so far.

2 _____
  _____

3 _____
  _____

4 _____
  _____

5 _____
  _____

My feet hurt. ①

I can't find my room key. ②

I'm really hungry. ③

I think Steve is angry with me. ④

I'm very wet! ⑤

88

3 VOCABULARY

Complete with these prepositions.

across from   behind   between   ~~in front of~~
inside   ~~near~~   next to   outside   over   under

1 The bicycle is _near_ the post office.
2 The police station is _____ the hotel.
3 The police car is _____ the hotel.

4 The thief is _in front of_ the bus.
5 The police car is _____ the bus.
6 The bus is _____ the thief and the police car.

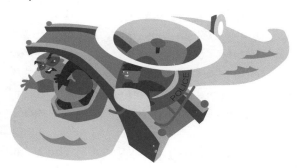

7 The helicopter is _____ the bridge.
8 The boat is _____ the bridge.

9 The thief is _____ the phone booth.
10 The police are _____ the phone booth.

4 VOCABULARY

Read the sentences and write responses. Use these phrases and suggest suitable places to go.

book a vacation   buy fruit   ~~buy some aspirin~~
ask for help   get a haircut   get a cold drink
buy a newspaper   buy some flowers

1 I have a headache.
You can _buy some aspirin at a drugstore._

2 I'm going to visit a friend in the hospital.
You can _____
_____

3 I'd like to know the baseball scores.
You can _____
_____

4 I want to visit Rio.
You can _____
_____

5 I'd like to eat an apple.
You can _____
_____

6 My hair is too long.
You can _____
_____

7 I can't find my car! It was here!
You can _____
_____

8 I'm hot and thirsty.
You can _____
_____

5 PRONUNCIATION

Circle the two rhyming words in each line.

1 (should)   food   (good)
2 flower   hour   your
3 wear   near   hair
4 eat   plate   great
5 crowd   road   loud
6 lost   post   most
7 first   worst   list
8 break   speak   shake

EXTENSION

Write a list of tips for tourists, like those in exercise 1, for your town or city.

3 **I LOVE GOING TO FESTIVALS**

1 READING

Read the interview with a music fan at Glastonbury Festival.

INTERVIEWER Sally, are you enjoying the festival?

SALLY Oh, yes. It's fantastic.

INTERVIEWER And what do you like most about it?

SALLY The music, of course, and the atmosphere. The people here are really friendly.

INTERVIEWER So you don't mind the rain?

SALLY Well, normally I don't like getting wet, but it's part of Glastonbury. So, no, I don't really mind waiting in line in the rain—or getting covered in mud. I love camping and I like getting up early, so I can always get to the front and see the bands up close.

INTERVIEWER And is there anything you don't like about the festival?

SALLY Yes, the trash. I can't stand it. Why can't people put it in the trash cans?

Now complete with these things.

camping   rain and mud   getting up early   trash

Sally …

1 can't stand _____.

2 doesn't mind _____.

3 likes _____.

4 loves _____.

2 GOOD/BAD AT + GERUND

Write sentences.

really good ☆☆   good ☆   bad ★

1 Sue/draw ☆
Sue's good at drawing.

2 Molly/play the guitar ☆☆
_____

3 David/remember things ★
_____

4 Jack/choose gifts ☆
_____

5 Harry/take pictures ☆☆
_____

6 Emily/tell jokes ★
_____

7 Maria/speak English ☆☆
_____

8 Beth/make friends ☆
_____

3 VERB + GERUND

What do Sam and Laura like doing? Complete the dialogue.

can't stand ✗   don't mind ✔   like ✔✔   love ✔✔✔

SAM I (**1**) _*can't stand going*_ (go ✗) to festivals.

LAURA Really? I (**2**) _____ (go ✔✔✔) to festivals. I go to two or three every year.

SAM I (**3**) _____ (camp ✗) in muddy fields.

LAURA Really? I (**4**) _____ (camp ✔✔). And I don't mind mud.

SAM And there are too many people. I don't like crowds. I (**5**) _____ (be ✔✔✔) alone.

LAURA Do you? I (**6**) _____ (be ✗) alone. I love the atmosphere in crowds.

SAM I also (**7**) _____ (wait ✗) in line in the rain.

LAURA I (**8**) _____ (wait ✔) in line in the rain. You meet a lot of great people. And then there's the music. I (**9**) _____ (hear ✔✔✔) new bands.

SAM Me too. But I can hear them on the radio.

LAURA Yes, but it's not the same.

SAM It's more comfortable. I (**10**) _____ (sit ✔✔) on the couch.

LAURA I (**11**) _____ (sit ✗) on the couch—it's so boring!

4 VERB/PREPOSITION + GERUND

Complete with the gerund of these verbs.

be   eat   listen   make   go   use   write   watch

1 I hate _____ mistakes.

2 Jake is good at _____ computers.

3 Do you like _____ sports on TV?

4 Kate can't stand _____ lost.

5 We enjoy _____ to hip-hop.

6 Sam is bad at _____ letters.

7 Georgie loves _____ burgers.

8 Is Grace interested in _____ to the concert?

5 VOCABULARY

Find eight music styles in the word square. Use the words to complete the sentences below.

C	A	J	H	G	E	M	U	R	C
H	E	A	V	Y	M	E	T	A	L
I	M	Z	O	L	E	L	E	P	T
P	U	Z	K	E	T	W	C	A	R
S	A	L	S	A	O	A	H	T	O
C	K	I	P	P	U	N	K	T	T
O	P	L	O	S	O	V	O	U	R
T	E	A	R	I	P	I	E	R	O
C	L	U	T	R	A	S	D	S	C
H	A	G	D	E	C	K	I	N	K

1 Jane plays the piano and the saxophone. Her favorite music is j *a z z*.

2 I don't like h __ __ __ __-m __ __ __ __. It's too noisy!

3 Look at Tim's hair and his clothes! You can see he likes p __ __ __ music.

4 R __ __ music is cool! It's like poetry with a strong beat.

5 I love dancing. Would you like to come to my s __ __ __ __ class next week?

6 My little sister likes p __ __ music, but I think it all sounds the same.

7 R __ __ __ music is my favorite! I'm learning to play the drums so I can be in a band.

8 "Do you like t __ __ __ __ __ music?" "No, I don't like electronic sounds."

6 VOCABULARY

Write the opposites. They are all in the text on page 28.

1 worse   *better*

2 love   _____

3 early   _____

4 found   _____

5 remember   _____

6 a little   _____

7 finishing   _____

8 back   _____

7 PRONUNCIATION

Do they rhyme (✔) or not (✗)?

1	else	tells	✗
2	cover	over	☐
3	kind	find	☐
4	lose	knows	☐
5	lost	cost	☐
6	rain	green	☐
7	wait	late	☐
8	love	move	☐
9	great	late	☐
10	crowd	loud	☐

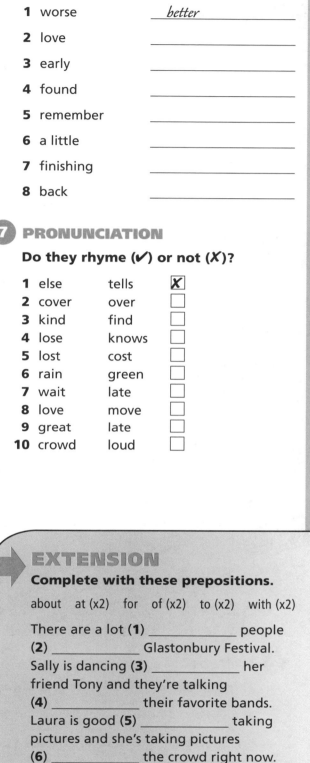

➡ EXTENSION

Complete with these prepositions.

about   at (x2)   for   of (x2)   to (x2)   with (x2)

There are a lot (**1**) _____ people (**2**) _____ Glastonbury Festival. Sally is dancing (**3**) _____ her friend Tony and they're talking (**4**) _____ their favorite bands. Laura is good (**5**) _____ taking pictures and she's taking pictures (**6**) _____ the crowd right now. Matt is talking (**7**) _____ Holly, and Sue is listening (**8**)_____ the music. Greg is looking (**9**) _____ his friends, Jade and Callum, but he can't see them. Is he angry (**10**) _____ them?

4 CELEBRATIONS
● Integrated Skills

1 READING

Read the text and complete with these phrases.

a goodbye to the old year
b to get more exercise
c of the Roman New Year
d and look forward to the future
e and at different times of the year
f bread, money, and coal

Different countries celebrate the new year in different ways (**1**) _e_ ! The Chinese New Year is in late January or February, the Jewish New Year is in September or October, and most Indian people celebrate the new year in the spring. But in many parts of the world, January 1 is New Year's Day. This is the original date (**2**) ____.

Although the new year starts on January 1 in many countries, it starts at different times because of international time zones. For example, the new year in Australia starts eighteen hours earlier than in San Francisco. People all over the world have parties on December 31—New Year's Eve. At midnight, they hold hands and sing *Auld Lang Syne*. This famous song, by the Scottish poet Robert Burns, says we should remember the past (**3**) ____.

The Scottish people have the best New Year's celebrations in the world, and New Year's Eve has a special name in Scotland: *Hogmanay*. People celebrate with bonfires and fireworks and in some towns they burn an old boat to say (**4**) ____. Many people in Scotland visit their friends after midnight, early on January 1. They believe that the first person to enter the home on New Year's Day can bring good luck. This person should bring gifts: (**5**) ____, so the family are not hungry, poor, or cold in the new year.

People everywhere have hopes for the new year and some make a list of New Year's resolutions: things they want to do or change. For example, they promise to be neater, to work harder, or (**6**) ____. But sometimes their resolutions don't last very long!

2 WRITING

Think of some resolutions you can make now! Think about:

your family   housework   money   friends   school   English

Write six sentences about things you should or shouldn't do.

I should go to bed earlier.

1 _____
2 _____
3 _____
4 _____
5 _____
6 _____

3 CROSSWORD

Complete the crossword puzzle.

(crossword grid with numbered cells 1–19)

ACROSS →
1. People in Brazil light … on New Year's Eve. (7)
4. You should go to … when you are tired. (3)
6. Opposite of *high*. (3)
7. New Year's Day is a national … in the U.S. (7)
8. The biggest country in South America. (6)
10. … easy to get lost at a carnival. (3)
13. In Thailand, New Year is … April. (2)
14. Opposite of *boring*. (8)
16. New Year's Eve is at the … of December. (3)
18. The Chinese … special food on New Year's Eve. (3)
19. In Thailand, people … water over each other! (5)

DOWN ↓
1. Different countries … the new year in different ways. (9)
2. At the present time. (3)
3. They … medicine at the drugstore. (4)
4. Emma is … … swimming and she doesn't enjoy it. (3, 2)
5. The weekend lasts for two … (4)
7. You can get a … at the hairdresser's. (7)
9. Sally and Perry … at a festival now. (3)
11. This is a road … (4)

12. Christina Aguilera is a pop … (4)
15. On January 1, people say, "Happy … Year!" (3)
17. … you like dancing? (2)

LEARNER INDEPENDENCE

LEARNING WORDS

Look at these words from the lesson and see how the parts of the words can help you remember them.

fireworks   grandparents   midnight
suitcase   underwear

For example, *underwear* contains the words *under* and *wear*. It's something you wear under something else.

UNIT 2   93

UNIT 2 FESTIVALS

Insights EXTRA!

CONSOLIDATION

1 Complete with comparative or superlative adjectives.

1 The Venice carnival is the _____ carnival in Italy. (romantic)

2 Glastonbury is the _____ music festival in Britain. (large)

3 Ramón is a _____ tennis player than Alex. (good)

4 The weather in Chicago is _____ than the weather in Mexico City. (bad)

5 Who is the _____ actor in the world? (popular)

6 Which sport is _____: soccer or volleyball? (exciting)

7 New York is the _____ city in the U.S. (big)

8 Jennifer Lopez is _____ than Norah Jones. (famous)

2 Look at the photo on page 26 and complete with these words.

behind   between   in front of   near   next to

1 Lara is standing _____ Ramón and Silvana.

2 Jay is standing _____ Silvana.

3 Silvana is standing _____ Lara.

4 Steve is standing _____ Ramón.

5 Silvana is standing _____ Jay.

Write the opposites.

1 over   _____

2 should   _____

3 behind   _____

4 outside   _____

5 cheap   _____

6 early   _____

3 Complete with the gerund of these verbs.

be   do   go   listen   meet   play   read   sleep   watch

1 She doesn't like _____ new people.

2 What things are you good at _____?

3 They can't stand _____ late.

4 We aren't interested in _____ TV.

5 He's bad at _____ soccer.

6 I don't enjoy _____ to parties.

7 What kind of music do you like _____ to?

8 She loves _____ in a tent.

9 What books do you like _____?

4 Complete the questions with *What, When, Who,* and *Where*. Then look at the text on page 30 and answer them.

1 _____ do people in Italy eat on New Year's Eve?

_____

2 _____ do people wear white clothes on New Year's Eve?

_____

3 _____ do they celebrate New Year's Eve in China?

_____

4 _____ wears yellow underwear on New Year's Eve?

_____

5 _____ do people throw on Thai New Year's Eve?

SPELLING

Correct the spelling of these words from Unit 2.

1 cel*e*ibrate   2 amasing   3 spectecular   4 esotic

5 noisyest   6 bigest   7 umbrela   8 medisine

9 intrested   10 croud   11 festaval   12 visiters

BRAINTEASER

A person lives on the tenth floor of a building. Every day he takes the elevator all the way down to the first floor. When he returns, he takes the elevator to the seventh floor and walks up the stairs to the tenth floor. He hates the stairs, so why does he walk up three floors?

Answer on page 97.

EXTENSION

1 Correct these sentences.

1 Holly thinks Glastonbury is the ~~better~~ *best* festival in the world.

2 The weather in Chicago is worst than the weather in Recife.

3 Which is the bestest soccer team?

4 Lady Gaga is a most exciting singer than Madonna.

5 New York is more bigger than Miami.

2 Read the sentences. Then write advice using these phrases, and *should* or *shouldn't*.

buy so many DVDs   write it down   leave home earlier
keep it in your bag   forget your homework

1 I'm always late for school.

You _____

2 I never have enough money.

You _____

3 I can never remember your phone number.

You _____

4 I can't find my dictionary again.

You _____

5 My teacher is angry.

You _____

3 Complete these sentences for you using the gerund.

1 I love _____

2 I hate _____

3 I'm good at _____

4 I'm bad at _____

5 I don't mind _____

6 I like _____

7 I don't like _____

8 I'm interested in _____

4 Write a paragraph in your notebook describing what happens when someone turns 18 in your country.

When someone turns 18 in my country, they have a big party. People eat ...

WEB WATCH

Look up Mardi Gras in New Orleans on the Internet and find out about the last carnival. Look up new words in the dictionary and make a *Carnival* section in your vocabulary notebook.

SPELLING

Complete the chart with these words. Then complete the rule.

~~call~~ ~~celebrate~~ center computer city
comparative circus costume cup once
dancer carnival December excuse cap

/k/	/s/
call	celebrate

Rule: The letter *c* is pronounced /k/ when it is followed by the letters ___ , ___ or *u*, and /s/ when it is followed by ___ or *i*.

BRAINTEASER

What is it that comes four times in every week, twice in every month, but only once in a year?

Answer on page 97.

Review 1 & 2

1 **Read and complete. For each number 1–16, choose word or phrase A, B, C, or D.**

NORTH AMERICAN FESTIVALS

One of the biggest festivals in the U.S. is the celebration of Independence Day on July 4. This is the __1__ important date in the history of the U.S.—it celebrates the American Declaration of Independence from Britain on July 4, 1776. Independence Day is a national holiday, and there __2__ huge parades with bands in cities and towns everywhere __3__ the U.S. It's summer, so the __4__ is usually nice and everyone is __5__ for the celebrations. There are parties in the streets and fantastic fireworks __6__ night.

Another very important day for Americans is Thanksgiving Day at the __7__ of November. This festival is from the early 17th century and everyone __8__ thanks that they have enough food. It is a traditional family day, with a delicious Thanksgiving __9__. In the days __10__ Thanksgiving, airports and roads are full because people travel to be with __11__ family. Visitors to the States in November __12__ to celebrate Thanksgiving with an American family.

To the north of the U.S., the people of Canada also celebrate Independence Day at the beginning of July. They __13__ exciting parades, parties, and special performances of plays and concerts. The Canadians celebrate Thanksgiving __14__ the Americans, on the second Monday in October. This is because winter __15__ earlier in Canada __16__ in the U.S.

1 A much	**B** too	**C** more	**D** most (circled)
2 A am	**B** is	**C** are	**D** be
3 A in	**B** under	**C** between	**D** near
4 A time	**B** weather	**C** sky	**D** sun
5 A inside	**B** outside	**C** home	**D** away
6 A in	**B** to	**C** at	**D** on
7 A last	**B** past	**C** first	**D** end
8 A give	**B** gives	**C** is giving	**D** are giving
9 A meals	**B** food	**C** dinner	**D** kitchen
10 A to	**B** before	**C** up	**D** with
11 A their	**B** there	**C** they	**D** theirs
12 A tries	**B** is trying	**C** should try	**D** shouldn't try
13 A are	**B** make	**C** have	**D** do
14 A before	**B** after	**C** later	**D** earlier
15 A begins	**B** is beginning	**C** ends	**D** is ending
16 A then	**B** than	**C** as	**D** when

2 **Complete with the correct form of the words in capitals.**

1 Pickpockets are a problem for ___tourists___ in lots of cities. TOUR

2 It is _____ to walk alone here at night. DANGER

3 The _____ play the different parts in a play or movie. ACT

4 Silvana and Ramón are two of the contest _____. WIN

5 Going to a carnival is really _____. EXCITE

6 *Auld Lang Syne* is a _____ Scottish song. TRADITION

7 What is your _____ kind of music? FAVOR

8 Are you _____ in sports? INTEREST

3 **Complete the second sentence so that it means the same as the first sentence.**

1 This isn't my jacket.
This jacket _isn't mine._

2 The girl is standing in front of the man.
The man _____

3 What's Steve's job?
What does _____

4 What clothes do you like wearing most?
What are _____

5 The restaurant is more expensive than the coffee shop.
The coffee shop _____
_____

6 The travel agency is over the flower shop.
The flower shop _____
_____

7 Alex is very good at dancing.
Alex isn't _____

8 I hate feeling cold.
I can't _____

4 **Find the word that's different.**

1 vet   teacher   singer   (sister)

2 jacket   jeans   pocket   shirt

3 chat   talk   sing   stand

4 bag   foot   hand   head

5 carnival   costume   festival   party

6 angry   funny   happy   worry

7 bread   champagne   coffee   wine

8 amazing   difficult   fantastic   spectacular

LEARNER INDEPENDENCE

SELF ASSESSMENT

A **Draw this chart in your notebook. How many words can you write in each category?**

More than 6? Good!
More than 8? Very good!
More than 10? Excellent!

Nationalities	
Clothes	
Colors	
Town facilities	

B **Put the words in order to make expressions from the phrasebooks in Lesson 4 in Units 1 and 2.**

1 not course of
Of course not.

2 me let see
_____

3 up now listen
_____

4 you hope I it like
_____

5 mean what you do
_____

6 safe it isn't
_____

7 you with coming I'm
_____

8 only problem the is …
_____

Check your answers.
8/8 Excellent!   *6/8* Very good!   *4/8* Try again!

MY LEARNING DIARY

In Units 1 and 2:
My favorite topic is _____
_____

My favorite picture is _____
_____

The three lessons I like most are _____
_____

My favorite activity or exercise is _____
_____

Something I don't understand is _____
_____

Something I want to learn more about is _____
_____

UNIT 3 — PAST TIMES

1 A FIRE STARTED AFTER THE EARTHQUAKE

1 READING

Read about the Great Fire of Rome and answer the questions.

1 Did the fire start in the day or at night?

_____

2 How did the flames get to the rest of the city?

_____

3 Where was Emperor Nero when the fire started?

_____

4 How did Emperor Nero help people?

_____

5 Why did Emperor Nero use stone and marble to rebuild the city?

_____

6 Why did people say that Emperor Nero started the fire?

_____

The Great Fire of Rome

The Great Fire of Rome started on the night of July 18, 64 AD in a store selling inflammable things. The wind quickly carried the flames to the rest of the city. The fire burned for five and a half days and it destroyed 70% of the city.

The historian Tacitus wrote that Emperor Nero returned from Actium to Rome when he heard about the fire. He helped look for people in the destroyed houses. He allowed people to stay in his palaces and he bought food for them. After the fire, he rebuilt the city with stone and marble – things which don't burn easily. He made the streets wide so that the wind couldn't carry flames from building to building.

But many people didn't like Nero. Some said he started the fire himself. Others said that he played the lyre (a musical instrument) and watched while Rome burned.

2 SIMPLE PAST OF BE

Complete with was/were or wasn't/weren't.

1 The Great Fire of Rome _____ in 64 AD.

2 When the fire started, Nero _____ in Rome.

3 The buildings _____ close together and there _____ a strong wind so the fire moved quickly.

4 After the fire, there _____ many buildings left in Rome.

5 When Nero rebuilt Rome, the buildings _____ stone and marble and the streets _____ wide.

3 SIMPLE PAST REGULAR VERBS

Add d or ed to make the simple past of these verbs.

borrow _ed_   like____   practice____

cause____   miss____   print____

discover____   design____   show____

help____   invent____   start____

Change the y to i and add ed to make the simple past of these verbs.

bury _____buried_____   study _____

carry _____   try _____

marry _____   worry _____

4 SIMPLE PAST IRREGULAR VERBS

Complete the chart.

Verb	Simple past	Verb	Simple past
begin	_began_	lose	
buy		make	
eat		meet	
find		put	
give		say	
go		send	
hear		sing	
hold		sit	
keep		speak	
know		throw	

5 SIMPLE PAST NEGATIVE

Complete with the simple past form of the verbs.

GREAT FIRE OF LONDON AGAIN

The Great Fire of London happened again yesterday, but it (**1**) _____ (not happen) in London. The fire was in the south-west of England and it (**2**) _____ (not be) an accident. Dave Kelly and his friends spent two years building a copy of London from 1666. "We (**3**) _____ (not build) all the city, of course," Dave said, "just a small part of it around Pudding Lane. We (**4**) _____ (not have) time to do more." Dave spent hours in the Museum of London. "We (**5**) _____ (not want) to make any mistakes," he said. The fire (**6**) _____ (not last) long—just a few minutes, but 20,000 people came to see it. Last year, Dave and his friends built a copy of a ship and a church and burned them. "But they (**7**) _____ (not be) as exciting as this," Dave said.

6 VOCABULARY

Write the years.

1   nineteen seventy-one _____ _1971_ _____
2   nineteen eighty-nine _____
3   nineteen ninety-eight _____
4   two thousand and two _____
5   1666   _sixteen sixty-six_ _____
6   1826   _____
7   1994   _____
8   2011   _____
9   2013   _____
10 2016   _____

7 VOCABULARY

Match these words with their definitions.

ballpoint pen   block   ~~cause~~   damage   flames
gold   helicopter   marry   smoke   spread

1   make something happen _____ _cause_ _____
2   when a man and a woman do this, they become husband and wife _____
3   move over a large area _____
4   a valuable, yellow metal _____
5   white, black, or gray cloud that comes from fire _____
6   have a bad effect _____
7   you see these when something burns _____
8   Igor Sikorsky invented it _____
9   you write with this _____
10 area of buildings with streets on all four sides _____

➡ EXTENSION

Correct these statements about what you did yesterday.

1   You got up at four o'clock in the morning.
    I didn't get up at four o'clock in the morning.
    I got up at _____
2   You had spaghetti for breakfast.
    _____
    _____
3   You wore your pajamas all day.
    _____
    _____
4   You watched a TV show about bees.
    _____
    _____
5   You had dinner at four o'clock.
    _____
    _____
6   You went to sleep at seven o'clock.
    _____
    _____

2 DID YOU HAVE FUN?

1 READING

Steve has given the students a quiz about California. Read the dialogue and match the years in list A with the things in list B.

SILVANA What's the first date?

ALEX 1542.

SILVANA James Marshall discovered gold?

ALEX No, that was in 1848.

SILVANA Yes, you're right. Is it when the first Europeans came to California?

ALEX Yes, that's it—1542. OK. When did California join the U.S. as the 31st state?

SILVANA Well, that was after James Marshall discovered gold. So, 1850?

ALEX Yes, I think that's right.

SILVANA OK. How about the movie industry? When did that start in Hollywood?

ALEX Oh, was that 1911 or 1927?

SILVANA I think that's 1911.

ALEX OK. And how about Arnold Schwarzenegger? Did he become Governor in 2003?

SILVANA Yes. And so, San Francisco International Airport obviously opened in 1927.

ALEX Great! We did it!

WORLD2DAY QUIZ

A		B	
a	1542	1	California joined the U.S. as the 31st state.
b	1848	2	San Francisco International Airport opened.
c	1850	3	The first Europeans came to California.
d	1911	4	Arnold Schwarzenegger became Governor of California.
e	1927	5	The movie industry started in Hollywood.
f	2003	6	James Marshall discovered gold in California.

2 SIMPLE PAST QUESTIONS

Complete with *Who, When,* or *What*.

1 _____ did California become a U.S. state?

2 _____ discovered gold?

3 _____ did the first Europeans come to California?

4 _____ did James Marshall discover in 1848?

5 _____ opened in 1927?

6 _____ did the movie industry in Hollywood start?

3 SIMPLE PAST QUESTIONS

Write questions for these answers.

1 The group went to the California Academy of Sciences. (Where?)
   Where did the group go?

2 At the academy they saw an exhibit. (What?)
   _____

3 They went to Nob Hill. (Where?)
   _____

4 After that, they visited a temple. (What?)
   _____

5 Emma had a drink outside. (What?)
   _____

6 The group met Alex in the park. (Who?)
   _____

4 SIMPLE PAST QUESTIONS AND SHORT ANSWERS

Write questions and short answers about what the group did this morning.

1 have fun   *Did they have fun?*   *Yes, they did.*

2 see a play   *Did they see a play?*   *No, they didn't.*

3 see an exhibit

_____

_____

4 climb up Nob Hill

_____

_____

5 all go inside the temple

_____

_____

6 meet Alex in the park

_____

_____

5 ADVERBIAL PHRASES OF TIME

Complete with *at*, *in*, or *on*.

1 _____ Sunday   5 _____ April

2 _____ the afternoon   6 _____ 4:15 a.m.

3 _____ noon   7 _____ June 11

4 _____ 1984   8 _____ Thursday evening

9 We use _____ before dates and days.

10 We use _____ before years and months.

11 We use _____ before *the morning/the afternoon/ the evening.*

12 We use _____ for clock times and before *night.*

6 VOCABULARY

Complete the chart with these adjectives from page 42. Two of the adjectives can go in both columns.

asleep   awesome   exhausted   great   hungry
spectacular   lazy   long   thirsty   steep

Adjectives for people	Adjectives for things
_____	_____
_____	_____
_____	_____
_____	_____
_____	_____
_____	

7 PRONUNCIATION

Say these words. Then cross out the silent letters.

exhibit   climb   science
design   exhausted   bought

➡ EXTENSION

Write questions about life 400 years ago and answer them.

1 go to the theater

Did people go to the theater then?
Yes, they did.

2 go to the movies

_____

_____

3 make phone calls

_____

_____

4 visit cathedrals

_____

_____

5 drive cars

_____

_____

6 have MP3 players

_____

_____

3 IT WAS COMING STRAIGHT TOWARD HIM

1 READING

Read about Josh Chapple and his meteorite.

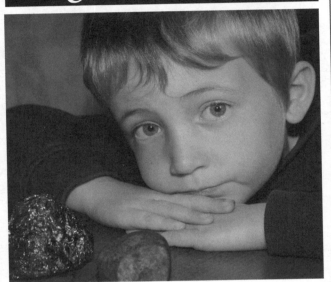

A gift from space

Josh Chapple, a six-year-old boy, was playing in his backyard when he found a black, shiny rock. He thought it was a meteorite, and a newspaper wrote a story about it. Meteorite collector, Robert Elliott, was looking at the newspaper's website when he saw the story. He knew immediately that Josh's rock wasn't a meteorite. However, he didn't want Josh to be disappointed, so he sent him a real meteorite. It was from the Sahara desert. A meteorite collector found it there in 1999. Josh was very happy when he received the gift. He said, "It's amazing—this has come all the way from space!"

Now read the sentences and write *T* (true) or *F* (false).

1 Josh was walking to school when he found a black, shiny rock. ☐

2 Robert Elliott wrote a story for the newspaper about Josh. ☐

3 Robert Elliott was on the computer when he heard about Josh's rock. ☐

4 Robert Elliott gave Josh a real meteorite because he didn't want him to be disappointed. ☐

5 Josh was happy because the meteorite came all the way from the Sahara desert. ☐

2 PAST PROGRESSIVE

What were the people doing when the accident happened?

~~wait for a bus~~   take a picture   eat a sandwich
look at a map   look at the camera   use a cell phone
drink a cup of coffee   read a newspaper

A _____was waiting for a bus._____

B _____

C _____

D _____

E _____

F _____

G _____

H _____

3 PAST PROGRESSIVE

Look at the photos on pages 42 and 43. Answer the questions.

1 Was Jay wearing a black T-shirt?

No, he wasn't. He was wearing a blue T-shirt.

2 Was Ramón standing in front of the Golden Gate Bridge?

_____

_____

3 Was Ramón standing next to Emma?

_____

_____

4 Was Emma wearing a pink top?

_____

_____

5 Was Emma standing in front of the cathedral with Ramón?

_____

_____

6 Was Jay standing near the cable car with Ramón?

_____

_____

4 PAST PROGRESSIVE QUESTIONS

Look at the photo on pages 10 and 11. Write questions for these answers.

1 *Was Emma telling everyone about San Francisco?*
No, Emma wasn't. Steve was telling everyone about San Francisco.

2 _____
No, Silvana wasn't. Lara was standing next to Steve.

3 _____
No, Ramón wasn't. Lara was holding a map.

4 _____
No, Alex wasn't. Jay was holding an umbrella.

5 _____
No, Emma wasn't. Silvana was helping Alex.

6 _____
No, Steve wasn't. The thin man was taking the wallet.

5 WHY? BECAUSE...

Write questions in the past progressive. Then answer them.

1 Ryan/feel/unhappy
Why was Ryan feeling unhappy?
he/lose/cell phone
Because he lost his cell phone.

2 you/run
_____
I/be/late
_____

3 Gerrit Blank/smile
_____
he/survive
_____

4 Josh/feel/happy
_____
he/get/a real meteorite
_____

5 Emma/sit/outside
_____
she/be/tired
_____

6 Alex/eat/ice cream
_____
he/be/hot
_____

6 VOCABULARY

Match the verbs in list A with the words and phrases in list B.

	A		B
1	ride	**a**	a story
2	wait	**b**	overboard
3	feel	**c**	for a bus
4	take	**d**	a bicycle
5	fall	**e**	a picture
6	survive	**f**	well
7	write	**g**	a river
8	cross	**h**	a meteorite strike

7 PRONUNCIATION

Mark the stressed syllable.

■

bicycle   emergency   transportation

helicopter   dangerous   spaceship

speedboat   enormous

 **EXTENSION**

Write three sentences about what you were doing when something else happened.

I was watching TV when the phone rang.

4 **BIOGRAPHY**
● Integrated Skills

1 READING

Read the story and complete with these words.

believe   disappeared   eyes   friends   ghosts   having   money   shouted   talking   wearing

A Christmas Carol

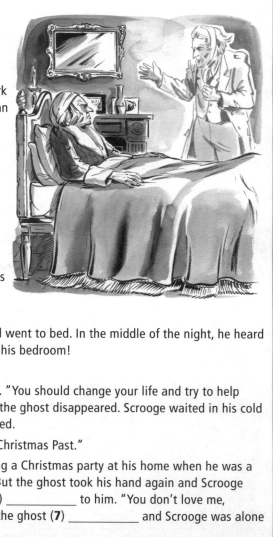

Charles Dickens wrote this famous story in 1843. It is about life in London at Christmas. There were many poor people in London then.

It was the day before Christmas and everyone was hard at work at the office of Ebenezer Scrooge. Scrooge was a cold, hard man who had no (**1**) _____. He only thought about money.

"Happy Christmas, Uncle!" shouted Fred, Scrooge's nephew.

"Nonsense!" Scrooge replied. "There is nothing happy about Christmas."

"Happy Christmas, Mr. Scrooge," said Bob Cratchit, who also worked in the office.

"I don't (**2**) _____ in Christmas!" Scrooge replied.

Then two men came to the office door. One of the men said, "You're a rich man. There are lots of poor people in London this Christmas. Can you give us some (**3**) _____ for them?"

"Get out!" shouted Scrooge. "I don't want to help the poor!"

Soon it was dark, and Scrooge went home to his big house and went to bed. In the middle of the night, he heard a noise and opened his (**4**) _____. There was a ghost in his bedroom!

"What do you want?" Scrooge (**5**) _____.

"I am here to tell you something important," the ghost replied. "You should change your life and try to help other people. Three other ghosts are coming to see you." Then the ghost disappeared. Scrooge waited in his cold bed. Then he heard a noise and a beautiful white ghost appeared.

"Come with me," the beautiful ghost said. "I am the ghost of Christmas Past."

The ghost took Scrooge's hand. Suddenly, Scrooge was watching a Christmas party at his home when he was a small child. Everyone was happy and Scrooge wanted to stay. But the ghost took his hand again and Scrooge saw himself as a young man. A beautiful young woman was (**6**) _____ to him. "You don't love me, Ebenezer, you only love money," the woman was saying. Then the ghost (**7**) _____ and Scrooge was alone in his bed. He felt very unhappy.

Later, another ghost visited Scrooge—the ghost of Christmas Present. He was (**8**) _____ a green coat. He took Scrooge to see the Christmas party at Bob Cratchit's house and at his nephew Fred's house. Everyone was (**9**) _____ fun … everyone except Scrooge.

A fourth ghost then came to see Scrooge. He was the ghost of Christmas Future and he was wearing black clothes. The ghost held Scrooge's hand and took him to a church. Outside the church, he saw his own name, EBENEZER SCROOGE, on a big stone.

"Is that me?" Scrooge asked. The ghost said "yes" and disappeared.

The next day, Scrooge was a different person. He got up early and he was singing and laughing. He bought Christmas gifts for everybody. He gave lots of money to the poor and he paid the workers in his office more money. "And all because of the (**10**) _____," Scrooge thought. "They showed me that people are more important than money."

2 READING

Read the sentences and write *T* (true) or *F* (false). Correct the false sentences.

1 No one was working in Scrooge's office. ☐ *F*

    Everyone was hard at work in Scrooge's office.

2 Bob Cratchit was Scrooge's nephew. ☐

_____

3 When Scrooge woke up, he saw a ghost in his bedroom. ☐

_____

4 "You shouldn't change your life," the first ghost said. ☐

_____

5 Four ghosts visited Scrooge. ☐

_____

6 "You only love money," the young woman was saying. ☐

_____

7 At the end of the story, Scrooge was happy. ☐

_____

3 CROSSWORD

Complete the crossword puzzle.

1		2			3	4				5	
				6							
		7				8				9	
10											
				11							
12			13						14		
					15		16				
17					18						

ACROSS →

1 Antonio Meucci made the first phone … (4)
3 Very well known. (6)
7 Emma's brother was at … in a sailboat when he fell overboard. (3)
8 Alex … lots of pictures. (5)
10 Opposite of *cold*. (3)
11 There was a Christmas … at Bob Cratchit's house. (5)
12 You write about your day in it. (5)
14 Infinitive of *was/were*. (2)
15 Someone with a lot of money is … (4)
17 Opposite of *early*. (4)
18 Jay was standing … to Lara. (4)

DOWN ↓

1 Large, important church. (9)
2 Opposite of *found*. (4)
4 Shakespeare was a well-known … and playwright. (5)
5 Lots of people … ballpoint pens to write with. (3)
6 We laugh when we are … (5)
9 In Shakespeare's time, there were … theaters in London. (7)
13 Simple past of *ride*. (4)
15 Simple past of *run*. (3)
16 Emma's brother fell overboard when the boat … a rock. (3)

LEARNER INDEPENDENCE

WORDS AND TOPICS

Grouping words by topic can help you remember them. Complete the chart with these words.

actor   bestseller   cathedral   church
diary   factory   novel   novelist   play
playwright   poem   reporter   story
teacher   theater   tower

Buildings	Occupations	Writing
_____	_____	_____
_____	_____	_____
_____	_____	_____
_____	_____	_____
_____	_____	_____

UNIT 3 PAST TIMES

Insights EXTRA!

CONSOLIDATION

1 Write sentences in the simple past.

1 Walt Disney/study English ✗/study art ✔

Walt Disney didn't study English. He studied art.

2 The San Francisco earthquake/happen in the day ✗/happen at night ✔

_____

_____

3 Silvana and Lara/go out ✔/stay in the hotel ✗

_____

4 László Biró/show the first movies ✗/invent the first ballpoint pen ✔

_____

_____

5 Gerrit Blank/find a meteorite ✔/find a ball ✗

_____

_____

6 Igor Sikorsky/invent the phone ✗/design the first helicopter ✔

_____

_____

2 Write questions and short answers.

1 San Francisco/burn down in 1966

Did San Francisco burn down in 1966?

No, it didn't.

2 Emma/visit the temple

_____

_____

3 Alex/go to the Golden Gate Bridge

_____

_____

4 Silvana and Jay/see an exhibit

_____

_____

5 the group/meet Alex in the park

_____

_____

6 Alex/sleep all morning

_____

_____

3 Write sentences using the past progressive + *when* + simple past.

1 Gerrit/walk/he/see a ball of light

Gerrit was walking when he saw a ball of light.

2 Josh/play in the yard/he/find a shiny, black rock

_____

_____

3 Emma's brother/sail/the boat/hit a rock

_____

_____

4 Ann Hodges/sleep/the meteorite/hit her house

_____

_____

5 Lara/run in the park/it/start to rain

_____

_____

6 Jay/chat online/the computer/stop working

_____

_____

4 Match the expressions with their meanings. Choose six from a–h.

1 It was awesome! | c |
2 It's extremely rare. | |
3 There was an enormous bang! | |
4 As far as we know… | |
5 She wasn't feeling well. | |
6 I'm really interested in it. | |

a We aren't sure.
b It took a long time.
c It was really great!
d I really like it.
e There aren't many.
f She was feeling sick.
g It's very expensive
h There was a very loud noise!

SPELLING

Complete these words from Unit 3 with the silent letters.

1 s__ience **2** b__ilding **3** well-__nown **4** lis__en
5 play__right **6** sc__ool **7** wa__king **8** __rote

BRAINTEASER

As long as I eat, I live. But when I drink, I die. What am I?

Answer on page 121.

EXTENSION

1 **Complete with the simple past of these verbs. You can use some verbs more than once.**

be   become   call   die   go   say   speak   want

Queen Elizabeth I
(**1**) _____ Queen of England for most of William Shakespeare's life. She (**2**) _____ born in London on September 7, 1533 and she (**3**) _____ Queen in 1558. Elizabeth (**4**) _____ several languages, including German, French, and Italian. Many men (**5**) _____ to marry her, but she always (**6**) _____ no, so people (**7**) _____ her the Virgin Queen. One of her men friends, Sir Walter Raleigh, (**8**) _____ to America in 1585 and (**9**) _____ the place Virginia after Elizabeth. Elizabeth's London (**10**) _____ very different from today's London, but some things (**11**) _____ the same. In 1586, Elizabeth prohibited soccer because of fighting at a soccer game! She (**12**) _____ in 1603 at the age of 70.

2 **Correct these questions. Then answer them.**

       discovered
1 Who ~~discover~~ gold in California in 1848?

_____

2 What were the date of the San Francisco earthquake?

_____

3 How many blocks did the fire destroyed?

_____

4 Who did make the world's first phone call?

_____

5 Where did the group saw an exhibit?

_____

6 What cathedral they visited?

_____

7 Do Emma go into the temple?

_____

8 Where they did meet Alex?

_____

3 **Write sentences about what you were doing at these times yesterday.**

At 7:30 a.m., I was sleeping.

7:30 a.m.

_____

9 a.m.

_____

1 p.m.

_____

3:30 p.m.

_____

6 p.m.

_____

9 p.m.

_____

10:30 p.m.

_____

4 **Write a biography of someone in your family in your notebook.**

WEB WATCH

Search the Internet to find out more about the life of an English-language writer, for example: Charles Dickens, Ernest Hemingway, Toni Morrison, John Steinbeck, Mark Twain, Virginia Woolf, William Shakespeare. Look up new words in the dictionary and make a *Biography* section in your vocabulary notebook.

SPELLING

Correct the spelling of these words from Unit 3 by doubling one or two letters in each word.

1 afternon **2** aslep **3** bestseler **4** balpoint
5 carton **6** colected **7** cel phone **8** hapy
9 hapen **10** hil **11** maried **12** midle
13 ocupation **14** sudenly **15** suces **16** swiming
17 spedboat **18** milion **19** feling

BRAINTEASER

Read the rhyme and answer the question.

When I was going to St. Ives,
I met a man with seven wives.
Every wife had seven sacks.
Every sack had seven cats.
Every cat had seven kittens.
Kittens, cats, sacks, and wives,
How many were going to St. Ives?

Answer on page 121.

① READING

Read *The world's most famous building* and complete the chart.

The world's most famous building

The Empire State Building opened in May 1931, and for 42 years it was the tallest building in the world. The twin towers of the World Trade Center, which opened in 1973, were taller than the Empire State Building, but terrorists destroyed the World Trade Center on September 11, 2001. The Empire State Building is 443 meters high and has 103 floors. It is taller than the Eiffel Tower in Paris (319 meters), the Great Pyramid of Giza in Egypt (107 meters), and Big Ben in London (67 meters).

At the top of the building, you can sometimes see snow and rain falling up because the air is very different at that height! And sometimes the rain is red!

There are 6,500 windows (washed twice a month) and 73 elevators. The high-speed elevators travel at up to 366 meters a minute. From the top, you can see more than 125 kilometers on a clear day. Over 2.5 million people visit the Empire State Building every year. Remember that there are often long lines for the elevators at the bottom of the building. And there are also long lines at the top—with people waiting to come down!

Empire State Building—the facts	
Opened	*May 1931*
Tallest building for	_____
Height	_____
Number of floors	_____
Number of windows	_____
Number of elevators	_____
Speed of elevators	_____
Visitors a year	_____

② WRITING

Use these facts to write a paragraph about the Chrysler Building in New York.

Chrysler Building—the facts			
Opened	May 1930	Number of windows	3,862
Tallest building for	one year	Number of elevators	32
Height	319 meters	Speed of elevators	213 meters a minute
Number of floors	77		

_____

_____

_____

_____

_____

Central Park

Central Park is an enormous park in the middle of New York City. It opened in 1859 and has more than four million trees and plants! 25 million visitors a year go there and you can see it in many movies and TV shows.

The park has several lakes and ponds, a zoo, places to sit, places where you can play sports, playgrounds for children, woods, and a theater. There are two ice-skating rinks. One of them becomes a swimming pool in July and August. The other becomes a garden. Many people, such as walkers, joggers, and cyclists, use the 10 kilometers of paths inside the park. On weekends and in the evenings after 7 p.m., the park is closed to cars. In the summer, the theater in Central Park has a Shakespeare festival and actors perform plays by Shakespeare. You can sometimes see famous actors and movie stars in these plays, and many of the tickets are free!

In the past, Central Park was a very dangerous place, especially at night when there were a lot of muggers—thieves who stole from people in the park and often injured them. Now the park has its own police officers. There are fewer crimes and the park is now pretty safe. But it is not a good idea to go there alone after dark!

3 READING

Read *Central Park*. Then read the sentences and write *T* (true) or *F* (false). Correct the false sentences.

1 Central Park is outside New York City. ☐

_____

2 The park has 25 million visitors a year. ☐

_____

3 You can ice-skate in the park in July and August. ☐

_____

4 You can't play sports in the park. ☐

_____

5 You can drive a car through the park on weekends. ☐

_____

6 It's always expensive to see a play in the park. ☐

_____

7 The actors in the plays are not well known. ☐

_____

8 It is usually safe to go to Central Park. ☐

_____

4 VOCABULARY

Match these words from the text with their definitions.

enormous   crimes   free   rink   injured
jogger   mugger   fewer   dangerous

1 bad activities, like stealing _____

2 someone who runs to keep fit _____

3 not safe _____

4 a thief who often hurts people _____

5 opposite of *more* _____

6 hurt _____

7 very big _____

8 a place for ice-skating _____

9 you don't have to pay _____

1 READING

Read the text. Then match the beginnings of the sentences with the endings.

Can animals see color?

Inside your eyes, there are "rods" and "cones." Rods allow you to see light and cones allow you to see colors. You have three sets of cones: those that see red, those that see blue, and those that see green. Your brain mixes these colors to make other colors. Not all animals are the same. For example, cats and dogs have many more rods in their eyes than you do. This means that they can see better than you at night and they are better at seeing moving things.

However, cats and dogs have only two sets of cones, so they can't see some colors. Cats aren't very good at seeing red. Dogs can't tell the difference between green and orange. To a dog, both these colors look more like gray. If you throw a bright orange tennis ball across a green field, a dog can follow it while it is moving. But when it stops, the dog may lose the ball against the background. So if you want to buy a ball for a dog, blue or yellow are good colors to choose.

1 If an animal has no cones in its eyes,

2 When a dog looks at an orange ball,

3 If you buy a ball for a dog,

4 If an animal has lots of rods,

5 If it is dark,

6 When a ball moves,

a a yellow ball is a good idea.

b it can't see colors.

c a cat sees better than a person.

d a dog can see it easily.

e it can see well in the dark.

f it sees a gray ball.

2 OPEN CONDITIONAL WITH IF/WHEN

Complete with these phrases.

go cycling   blow the whistle
get a good picture   go on vacation

1 Hold the camera still if you want to

_____.

2 Always wear a helmet when you

_____.

3 Don't take too many clothes when you _____.

4 Stop playing when I _____

_____.

3 OPEN CONDITIONAL WITH IF/WHEN

Match the beginnings of the sentences with the endings.

1 When you use a digital camera, you `b`

2 If you want to check a digital picture immediately, you ☐

3 If you don't like a digital picture, you ☐

4 If you have a printer, you ☐

5 If you take digital pictures, it's easy to ☐

6 If you have a traditional camera, you ☐

a can print digital pictures at home.

b don't need any film.

c e-mail them to people.

d can look at it in the camera.

e have to wait to see your pictures.

f can delete it.

4 VOCABULARY

Match the words in list A with the words in list B to make six compound words. Then write the words.

	A	B		
1	computer	guide	1	_____
2	ice	phone	2	_____
3	digital	color	3	_____
4	camera	cream	4	_____
5	tour	chip	5	_____
6	primary	camera	6	_____

5 VOCABULARY

The same letter is missing in each line. Write the complete words.

1 blak   calulation   piture   sience

_____

2 anwer   brightnes   intant   proces

_____

3 digitl   mesure   primry   usully

_____

4 langage   nervos   compter   troble

_____

5 ligt   matematics   poto   wite

_____

6 VOCABULARY

Complete with these words.

angry   happy   nervous   rude   simple   terrible

1 She's smiling and looks really _____.

2 I feel _____. My head hurts a lot and I'm really hot and tired.

3 Steve's very _____—I've never seen him in a bad mood before.

4 All you have to do is press here. It's very _____.

5 Everyone gets _____ before tests.

6 When someone asks you a question, it's _____ not to answer.

7 PRONUNCIATION

Do they rhyme (✔) or not (✗)?

1	share	sure	✗
2	food	good	☐
3	friend	send	☐
4	green	screen	☐
5	watch	match	☐
6	square	chair	☐
7	bright	white	☐
8	great	meet	☐
9	phone	one	☐

EXTENSION

Complete these sentences for you.

1 I feel nervous when _____

_____

2 I feel happy if _____

_____

3 I like it when _____

_____

4 I feel angry when _____

_____

5 I feel good if I _____

_____

6 I don't like it when _____

_____

UNIT 4

SOUND AND VISION

2 WHICH WILL WE CHOOSE?

1 READING

Read the dialogue. Then read the sentences and write *T* (true) or *F* (false).

SILVANA It's Lara's birthday tomorrow. Let's buy her a gift.

ALEX Good idea. But what?

SILVANA She likes music. How about a CD?

ALEX Does she have a CD player?

SILVANA Not here, but she has one at home. She brought her MP3 player with her.

ALEX Let's buy her a CD. Then she can listen to it at home and put the songs on her MP3 player, too.

SILVANA What kind of music does she like?

ALEX She was listening to Amy Macdonald yesterday. She let me listen to some of it and it was really nice. I think she likes female singers. But she already has all of Amy Macdonald's albums.

SILVANA There's a new Katie Melua album out now.

ALEX Yes, I think that's a good idea. I like Katie Melua too.

SILVANA Oh, Alex. It's a gift for Lara, not you!

ALEX Yes, I know, but maybe she will let me listen to it.

1 Silvana and Alex are going to buy a gift for Lara. ☐

2 Lara has an MP3 player in the U.S. ☐

3 Lara has a CD player in the U.S. ☐

4 Alex likes Amy Macdonald. ☐

5 Silvana and Alex are going to buy Lara an Amy Macdonald album. ☐

6 Alex is going to buy a Katie Melua album for himself. ☐

2 *WILL/WON'T*: FUTURE PREDICTIONS

Write questions and short answers about the rest of the World2day vacation.

1 the group/go inside Alcatraz ✗

   Will the group go inside Alcatraz? — — — — — *No, they won't.*

2 they/take a boat trip ✔

   _____   _____

3 Emma/have a surprise ✔

   _____   _____

4 Jay/lose his phone ✗

   _____   _____

5 Lara and Alex/make a video ✔

   _____   _____

6 the weather/be bad ✗

   _____   _____

Now write sentences.

1 *The group won't go inside Alcatraz.* _____

2 _____

3 _____

4 _____

5 _____

6 _____

112

3 WILL/WON'T: FUTURE PREDICTIONS

Complete with *will* or *won't* and these phrases.

win the game   get some nice gifts   catch the last bus
come to school   forget anything   tell anyone

1 It's Jessica's birthday. I'm sure she _____
_____.

2 Don't worry, I _____
_____ your secret.

3 Make a shopping list. Then you _____
_____.

4 Let's call a taxi. I don't think we _____
_____.

5 John isn't feeling well today. I don't think he _____
_____ tomorrow.

6 Our team is awesome! I'm sure we _____
_____.

4 VOCABULARY

Complete with these words.

expensive   download   available
popular   replaced   introduced

1 Lots of people listen to his music—he's very
_____.

2 Sony _____ the Walkman in 1979.

3 At first, CDs were very _____, but
now they're much cheaper.

4 Today many people _____ music
from the Internet.

5 CDs have now _____ cassette tapes.

6 Although tape recorders were invented in 1928,
they weren't _____ in the U.S. until
the 1940s.

5 PRONUNCIATION

Complete the chart with these words.

~~listen~~   ~~invent~~   record (*noun*)   record (*verb*)
cassette   answer   money   replace
surprise   album   prefer   appear

■■	■■
listen	*invent*

6 VOCABULARY

Label the pictures with these words.

cassette tape   LP   cylinder   MP3 player   CD

1 _____   2 _____

3 _____   4 _____

5 _____

→ EXTENSION

**Put the words in the right order
to make questions. Then answer
the questions for you. If you aren't
sure, use *I think ...* or *Maybe ...***

1 be you when 21 will

Q _____ ?
A _____

2 tomorrow time what will up you get

Q _____ ?
A _____

3 will lunch you what tomorrow
for have

Q _____ ?
A _____

4 Sunday be where on you will morning

Q _____ ?
A _____

3 YOU SPOKE TOO FAST

1 READING

Read the story and complete with adverbs of manner.

Last week, a young man walked into a bank. He looked around (**1**) _____ (nervous) and then (**2**) _____ (quick) gave an envelope to the woman there.

The woman looked (**3**) _____ (careful) at the envelope and its message: GIVE ME ALL THE MONEY! I HAVE A GUN! Then she looked up at the man, who was now pointing a gun at her! So the woman (**4**) _____ (quiet) handed over all the money, and the thief put it in his bag and left the bank smiling (**5**) _____ (happy).

The thief soon got home and started counting his money. (**6**) _____ (sudden), the door opened and the police appeared. The thief (**7**) _____ (immediate) put his hands up. "But I don't understand!" he said (**8**) _____ (sad). "How did you find me so (**9**) _____ (fast)?" "Very (**10**) _____ (easy)," replied the police officer. "Your name and address were on the other side of the envelope."

2 ADVERBS OF MANNER

Complete the chart.

Adjective	Adverb
bad	bad**ly**
correct	
honest	
loud	
rude	
slow	
angry	ang**ily**
bossy	
hungry	
comfortable	comfortab**ly**
terrible	
beautiful	beautiful**ly**
special	
successful	

3 ADVERBS OF MANNER

Complete with adverbs from the chart in exercise 2.

1 I miss my family _____ when I'm away from home.

2 Emma shouldn't speak so _____ to Steve.

3 Jay wanted something to eat and looked at the pizza _____.

4 "Sssh! Don't talk so _____ in the studio."

5 Silvana was walking _____ because her feet hurt.

6 Great! You answered all the questions _____.

7 The concert was amazing! The girl played the violin _____.

8 The director thinks the group acted _____, but I think they acted well.

Now write six more sentences using the other adverbs from the chart.

_____

_____

_____

_____

_____

_____

4 READING

Read about Jay's favorite TV show and complete with these prepositions.

about   at   for   from   in   of   on   to   with (x2)

"My favorite show is called *Numbers*—it's (**1**) _____ TV (**2**) _____ an hour every Friday and ten million people watch the show every week. *Numbers* is set (**3**) _____ Los Angeles. It's (**4**) _____ a brilliant math professor named Charlie who helps his brother Don, an FBI agent, fight crime using math. Each episode begins (**5**) _____ a crime which Don and his team investigate. They then ask Charlie to help them and he uses math to find the criminal. It's very interesting, even if you aren't good (**6**) _____ math. One (**7**) _____ my favorite characters is Amita, a math professor (**8**) _____ India. She is married (**9**) _____ Charlie. They live (**10**) _____ Alan, who is Don and Charlie's father."

5 VOCABULARY

Which of these adverbs can follow all the verbs/phrases in each line?

hard   high   ~~late~~   long   well

1	stay up	get up	go to bed	*late*
2	work	try	think	_____
3	feel	do	sleep	_____
4	fly	jump	reach	_____
5	wait	stay	live	_____

6 VOCABULARY

Complete Steve's instructions with these words.

adverb   bodies   drama   easy   exercise   important   like   move   ready   run   talk   voices

"Here are two (**1**) _____ exercises for your (**2**) _____ and voices. These exercises are quick, (**3**) _____, and a lot of fun. Are you (**4**) _____ for the first one? It's for your bodies. I want you to (**5**) _____ around the room in the way that I tell you. For example, when I give you the (**6**) _____ "quickly," I want you to (**7**) _____ around the room. Is that clear?

The second (**8**) _____ uses your (**9**) _____. I'll give you an adverb, for example, "happily," and I want you to (**10**) _____ in that way. You can say anything you (**11**) _____—it's how you say it that is (**12**) _____."

7 CROSSWORD

Complete the crossword puzzle and find the mystery word ↓ .

1 An actor's role in a movie or play.
2 This person tells the actors what to do.
3 You can watch plays here.
4 One part of a play or movie.
5 Someone who plays a role in a movie or play.
6 Actors do lots of … exercises.
7 A performance of a play or musical event.
8 The actor felt very … when he got a big part in the movie.
9 William Shakespeare wrote lots of …

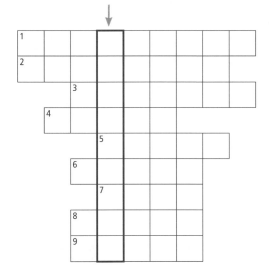

EXTENSION

Think of an actor you like. Write a paragraph in your notebook about how he/she acts. Use adverbs from this lesson.

UNIT 4

4 TV SHOWS
● Integrated Skills

1 READING

Read this description of a favorite movie and complete with these words.

answer   friends   parents   place   police   popular   questions   school   watches   wins

SLUMDOG MILLIONAIRE

One of my favorite movies is *Slumdog Millionaire*. Danny Boyle directed the movie and it won eight Oscars. I think it will become one of the most (**1**) _____ movies of all time because it is such a good story. It takes (**2**) _____ in Mumbai in India. It's about a boy named Jamal Malik. He has no father and his mother dies when he is five. Jamal and his brother, Salim, grow up in a big slum—a place where thousands of very poor people live together. It is very dirty there and life is hard and dangerous. Jamal makes (**3**) _____ with a little girl named Latika. She also has no (**4**) _____. They grow up together, but bad men take Latika away. She has to work for a man named Javed. He uses poor people to make money. Salim works for him too. Many years later, Jamal goes on the TV show *Who Wants to Be a Millionaire*? He doesn't know where

Latika is, but he knows that she (**5**) _____ the show. He answers nine (**6**) _____ correctly. Before he answers the tenth question, the police take him away. No one believes that a poor boy who has never been to (**7**) _____ can answer such difficult questions correctly. They think someone is helping him. Jamal explains how he knows the answers. Each question is connected to something that has happened in his life. The (**8**) _____ believe him and let him go. Back on the show, Jamal doesn't know the (**9**) _____ to the tenth question, but he is allowed to call a friend. He calls Salim, but Salim gives his cell phone to Latika. Latika doesn't know the answer to the question either, so Jamal guesses. He guesses the correct answer and (**10**) _____ a lot of money. At the end of the movie, he and Latika go away together.

2 VOCABULARY

Complete with these words from the text.

slum   explain   allow   grow up   favorite   correct

1 Your _____ movie is the one you like best.

2 Children _____ and become adults.

3 A _____ is a place where a lot of very poor people live.

4 A _____ answer to a question is the right answer.

5 If you _____ someone to do something, you let them do it.

6 To _____ something is to say how it happens.

3 WRITING

Think about one of your favorite movies and complete this summary.

One of my favorite movies is _____.

It takes place in _____.

It's about _____

_____

_____.

At the end of the movie, _____

_____.

4 CROSSWORD

Complete the crossword puzzle.

1		2		3		4		5		6
								7		
8						9				
10								11		
						12				
13				14	15		16			
			17							
	18									

ACROSS ➡
1 When you ... someone, you ask them lots of questions. (9)
7 You use this to listen. (3)
8 I live in a house, but my friends live in an ... (9)
10 Drums and guitars are musical ... (11)
12 The group wants to ... some drama exercises. (2)
13 Shakespeare lived a long time ... (3)
14 You can print digital photos ... home. (2)
16 The director thinks they spoke ... fast. (3)
18 Happen. (4, 5)

DOWN ⬇
1 Not real. (9)
2 Cars, buses, and trains are all kinds of ...ation (9)
3 Come back. (6)
4 ...-skating rink. (3)
5 Opposite of *dry*. (3)
6 You can buy medicine here. (9)
9 I'm very tired—I ... a vacation badly! (4)
11 won't = will ... (3)
15 Opposite of *bottom*. (3)
17 All right. (2)

LEARNER INDEPENDENCE

WORD COMBINATIONS

The verbs *make* and *take* go with different words. Make word maps with these words.

a̶ b̶u̶s̶   a cake   a break   a movie   friends   a list
place   a phone call   a shower   a picture   sure

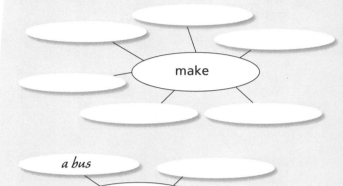

SOUND AND VISION

Insights EXTRA!

CONSOLIDATION

1 **Match the beginnings of the sentences with the endings.**

1 You feel good ☐
2 You feel sad ☐
3 You get angry ☐
4 You get tired ☐
5 You get wet ☐
6 You feel nervous ☐
7 You feel silly ☐
8 You feel very sick ☐

a when you hear some bad news about a friend.

b if you're out in the rain.

c when someone remembers your birthday.

d if someone is very rude to you.

e if you do too much.

f if you make a mistake in front of other people.

g if you drink water from the ocean.

h when you do something important for the first time.

2 **Complete the dialogue with 'll/will or won't.**

Silvana talks to her mom before she goes to the U.S.

SILVANA I hope I **(1)** _'ll_ meet some nice people when I'm in the U.S.

MOM Sure you **(2)** _____. I know you **(3)** _____ have a lot of fun.

SILVANA But I expect I **(4)** _____ hate the food.

MOM No, you **(5)** _____!

SILVANA And I hope it **(6)** _____ rain.

MOM I'm sure it **(7)** _____!

SILVANA **(8)** _____ you call me?

MOM Yes, but I'm sure you **(9)** _____ have time to talk to me!

3 **Complete with adverbs of manner from these adjectives.**

good   late   loud   polite   quick   sad

1 "Come here!" Steve shouted _____.

2 Jay got up _____ and didn't catch the bus.

3 "Excuse me," Lara said _____. "Can you help me?"

4 Steve thought the group did very _____ in the movie.

5 "It'll soon be time to go home," Ramón said _____.

6 Alex did the crossword _____, but he made some mistakes.

4 **Complete the questions about *The Simpsons* with these words. Then answer them.**

What (x2)   Where   When   How many

1 _____ does it take place?

_____

2 _____ countries is it shown in?

_____

3 _____ is it about?

_____

4 _____ color are the Simpsons?

_____

5 _____ was the show first broadcast?

_____

SPELLING

Complete these words from Unit 4 with vowels.

1 ch__r__ct__r   2 d__c__m__nt__ry
3 __m__rg__ncy   4 __p__s__d__
5 __x__rc__s__   6 n__rv__ __sly
7 p__rf__rm__nc__   8 r__h__ __rs__l
9 c__lc__l__t__ __n   10 thr__ll__r

BRAINTEASER

What is always in front of you, but you can never see it?

Answer on page 121.

1 **Complete the sentences for you.**

1 I always get excited when ___it's my birthday.___

2 If I'm rude to someone, I _____

3 I love it when people _____

4 If I lose my temper, I _____

5 I hate it when a stranger _____

6 I never hide my feelings when _____

7 If I'm by myself, I often _____

8 If someone gives me a surprise, I _____

2 **Complete these predictions with *will* or *won't* and your own words.**

1 She went to live in Australia, but I'm sure that we _____

_____

2 I'm going to watch the next episode. What do you think _____

_____

3 I hate soccer, so I definitely _____

_____

4 She's learning to ski—I hope that she _____

_____

5 I don't think I _____ because I'm too tired.

3 **Complete with the correct form of these verbs, plus an adverb.**

Verbs arrive rehearse shout sleep work
Adverbs angrily early hard properly well

1 I feel great. I _____ very _____ last night.

2 I'm sure that she'll pass her exams. She always _____ very _____.

3 What was the matter with Emma last night? She _____ at Jay several times.

4 They want to give a good performance. They know it's important to _____.

5 What a surprise! Alex usually arrives late, but today he _____ ten minutes _____.

4 **Write a paragraph in your notebook describing an imaginary TV soap. Say who is in it, where it takes place, and predict what will happen in the next episode.**

WEB WATCH

Look for your favorite American TV show on the Internet. Look up new words in the dictionary and make a *TV* section in your vocabulary notebook.

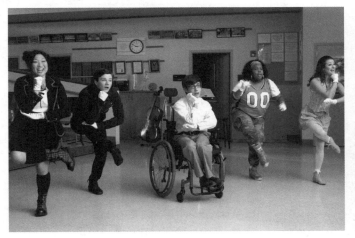

SPELLING

The letters *ch* can be pronounced /k/ or /tʃ/. Complete the chart with these words.

chair character change charge chat cheese child
China chips chocolate choose Christmas church
each lunch schedule school teacher techno which

/k/	/tʃ/	
_____	_____	_____
_____	_____	_____
_____	_____	_____
_____	_____	_____
_____	_____	_____
	_____	_____
	_____	_____
	_____	

BRAINTEASER

A doctor and a boy are fishing. The boy is the doctor's son, but the doctor isn't the boy's father. Who is the doctor?

Answers on page 121.

Review UNIT 3 & UNIT 4

1 **Read about Roman London. Then read the sentences and choose *True*, *False*, or *Doesn't say*.**

Female Gladiators

The Romans built a spectacular amphitheater in the city of London, England in 70 AD. It was about 100 meters long and 85 meters wide. In 200 AD, up to 7,000 people watched gladiators in the amphitheater. At that time, only 20,000 people lived in the city, so there was room in the amphitheater for one in three inhabitants! There were fights every month, and now we know that one of the gladiators was a woman—a gladiatrix.

In 1996, workers found the burned skeleton of a woman gladiator in London, near the river Thames. The date of the skeleton was 100–200 AD, and with it there was a picture of a gladiator.

Simon Thurley, Director of the Museum of London, said, "From the picture and other things we found with the skeleton, we think that this is our first skeleton of a gladiatrix. She was about 20. I hope that we will find more skeletons like it. We know that women gladiators were very popular in Roman times, but the Emperor Septimius Severus prohibited them in 200 AD."

Dr. Mary Beard of the University of Cambridge was surprised. "There are lots of pictures of Roman gladiators. One picture doesn't mean that this skeleton is a gladiatrix," she said.

1 Fire destroyed the Roman amphitheater.
  A True   **B** False   **C** Doesn't say

2 The population of London in Roman times was 7,000.
  A True   **B** False   **C** Doesn't say

3 Archaeologists found a picture of a gladiator with the skeleton.
  A True   **B** False   **C** Doesn't say

4 The gladiatrix fought near the river.
  A True   **B** False   **C** Doesn't say

5 Simon Thurley found the skeleton.
  A True   **B** False   **C** Doesn't say

6 Simon Thurley says they are going to find more skeletons like it.
  A True   **B** False   **C** Doesn't say

7 Emperor Septimius Severus prohibited women gladiators in 200 AD.
  A True   **B** False   **C** Doesn't say

8 Dr. Mary Beard wants to see the skeleton.
  A True   **B** False   **C** Doesn't say

9 Dr. Mary Beard says the skeleton is definitely not a gladiatrix.
  A True   **B** False   **C** Doesn't say

2 **Complete with the correct form of the words in capitals.**

1 The group was _____ after the sightseeing tour. EXHAUST

2 The San Francisco earthquake destroyed hundreds of _____. BUILD

3 The actors had a _____ in the TV studio. REHEARSE

4 Shakespeare is one of the world's most famous _____. PLAY

5 Charles Dickens was the most popular _____ of his time. WRITE

6 The _____ of the telephone changed people's lives. INVENT

7 Emma sometimes talks _____. ANGRY

8 *Avatar* is one of the most _____ movies of all time. SUCCESS

9 Soaps aren't real—they're _____. IMAGINE

10 Will Emma and Steve have an _____? ARGUE

3 Complete the second sentence so that it means the same as the first sentence.

1 The people of San Francisco were asleep when the earthquake started.
When the earthquake *started, the people of San Francisco were* asleep.

2 The first person to travel in space was Yuri Gagarin.
Yuri Gagarin _____
_____

3 You get green when you mix blue and yellow paint.
If _____
_____

4 When Alex arrived, everyone was already eating lunch.
Everyone _____
_____

5 Ryan was sailing with a friend when he fell overboard.
When Ryan _____
_____

6 Kafka is one of the world's most famous writers.
Kafka _____
_____ world.

7 We won't find out what happens until the next episode.
We'll find out _____
_____

8 I'm sure that *The Simpsons* won't end next year.
I really don't think that _____
_____

4 Find the word that's different.

1 (bridge) church museum store
2 helicopter plane ship spaceship
3 exhausted expensive lazy tired
4 angrily badly politely rudely
5 accident emergency success tragedy
6 doctor hospital nurse patient

ANSWERS TO BRAINTEASERS

UNIT 3
Consolidation **A fire.**
Extension **One person (the speaker).**

UNIT 4
Consolidation **The future.**
Extension **The boy's mother.**

LEARNER INDEPENDENCE

SELF ASSESSMENT

A Draw this chart in your notebook. How many words can you write in each category?

More than 6? Good!
More than 8? Very good!
More than 10? Excellent!

Transportation	
Jobs and occupations	
Adverbs of manner	
TV shows	

B Put the words in order to make expressions from the phrasebooks in Lesson 4 in Units 3 and 4.

1 fun did have you
_____

2 understand don't I
_____

3 bad that's too oh
_____

4 awesome it was
_____

5 feeling she wasn't well
_____

6 sense doesn't make it
_____

7 I news bad have some
_____

8 happened you what to
_____

Check your answers.

8/8 Excellent! *6/8* Very good! *4/8* Try again!

MY LEARNING DIARY

In Units 3 and 4:
My favorite topic is _____
_____

My favorite picture is _____
_____

The three lessons I like most are _____
_____

My favorite activity or exercise is _____
_____

Something I want to learn more about is _____
_____

121

Word List

The Word List excludes most of the vocabulary from *Insights 1* and *2*. The numbered reference after each word is to the lesson where the word first occurs. e.g.:

2.3 = Unit 2 Lesson 3
1C = Unit 1 Culture

adj = adjective
adv = adverb
conj = conjunction
det = determiner
n = noun
prep = preposition
pron = pronoun
v = verb

a long way (from)	2.3
able (be able to) (adj)	2.3
above (prep)	1C
accident (n)	4.4
account (n)	1.3
across from (prep)	2.2
acting company (n)	3.4
actor (n)	1.3
actually (adv)	3.3
add (v)	1.3
adjective (n)	4.4
adverb (n)	4.4
advertising sign (n)	1C
afraid (of) (adj)	4.2
after (prep)	1.1
afternoon (n)	3.2
afterward (adv)	3.3
ago (prep)	3C
agree (v)	2.2
angrily (adv)	4.3
angry (adj)	1.4
appear (v)	4.2
aquarium (n)	1C
arrival (n)	2.4
art school (n)	3.1
asleep (adj)	3.1
astronaut (n)	1C
at first (adv)	3.3
atmosphere (n)	2.3
available (adj)	4.2
awesome (adj)	1C
backstage (adv)	2.3
bad (at) (adj)	2.3
badly (adv)	3.1
bag (n)	1.2
ball (n)	
1 = dance	2.1
2 = round object	3.3
ballpoint pen (n)	3.1
band (n)	1.3
bang (n)	3.3
bank (n)	2.2
beautiful (adj)	1C
become (v)	3.1
behind (prep)	1.2
bell (n)	2.4
bestseller (n)	3.4

between (*place*) (prep)	1C
between (*time*) (prep)	3.2
bicycle (n)	3.3
block (n)	3.1
boat (n)	1C
book (v)	2.2
bookstore (n)	2.2
border (n)	1C
born (adj)	3.1
boss (n)	1.3
bottom (n)	1C
brightness (n)	4.1
bring (v)	2.3
broadcast (n)	4.4
broadcast (v)	1.3
build (v)	3.1
building (n)	3.1
burger (n)	2.3
burn (v)	2.4
burn up (v)	3.3
bus (n)	1C
businessman (n)	4.4
button (n)	4.1
cable car (n)	2.2
calculation (n)	4.1
camera (n)	1.2
camp (v)	2.3
candle (n)	2.4
canyon (n)	1C
car (n)	3.1
career (n)	3.4
carefully (adv)	4.3
carnival (n)	2.1
cartoon (n)	3.1
case (= example) (n)	3.3
cassette (n)	4.2
cathedral (n)	3.2
cause (v)	3.1
CD (compact disc) (n)	4.2
celebrate (v)	2.1
celebration (n)	2.4
cell phone (n)	1.3
champagne (n)	2.4
chance (n)	3.3
change money	2.2
character (e.g. letter) (n)	1.3
character (*person*) (n)	4.3
chat (v)	1.1
cheap (adj)	2.1
cheek (*face*) (n)	2.2
Christmas	1C
church (n)	2.4
circus (n)	1C
classmate (n)	3.3
climb (v)	3.2
close (adj)	2.3
clothes (n)	1.2
coffee shop (n)	2.2
collect (v)	3.4
colorful (adj)	2.1
community (n)	3.2
company (n)	1C
compare (v)	4.1

complete (adj)	1C
computer chip (n)	4.1
concert (n)	4.3
contact (n)	2.3
contain (v)	3.3
continue (v)	3.4
cool (adj)	2.1
cosmopolitan (adj)	2.1
costume (n)	2.1
cover (v)	1C
crazy (adj)	4.3
create (v)	1.3
creature (n)	1C
crowd (n)	2.1
crowded (adj)	1C
cylinder (n)	4.2
damage (n & v)	3.1
dancer (n)	2.1
dangerous (adj)	2.1
day (n)	1.3
deal (v)	4.4
death (n)	3.4
decision (n)	4.4
deep (adj)	1C
delete (v)	4.1
depend (It depends.) (v)	1.4
design (v)	3.1
destroy (v)	3.1
digital photo (n)	4.1
director (n)	4.3
disc (n)	4.2
doctor (n)	1.3
documentary (n)	4.4
downtown (adj)	3.1
dragon (n)	2.4
drama (n)	4.3
dress (n)	1.4
drugstore (n)	2.2
drummer (n)	2.1
dry (adj)	2.1
during (prep)	2.1
e-mail address (n)	1.3
early (adv)	2.2
earn money	2.3
earthquake (n)	3.1
easily (adv)	4.4
effect (n)	2.1
emergency (n)	3.3
enormous (adj)	3.3
enough (adv)	3.3
enough (det)	4.3
entrance (n)	1C
envelope (n)	2.4
episode (n)	4.4
escape (n)	3.3
escape (v)	4.4
evening (n)	1.4
exactly (adv)	3.4
exciting (adj)	1C
exhausted (adj)	3.2
exhibit (n)	3.2
exotic (adj)	2.1
expensive (adj)	2.1
expert (n)	3.3

explorer (n)	3C
extraordinary (adj)	4.4
extremely (adv)	3.1
factory (n)	3.4
fall (v)	3.3
falls (n pl)	1C
fame (n)	3.4
fan (*person*) (n)	2.3
far (adj)	1.1
fashion (n)	4.4
fashionable (adj)	4.4
fast (adv)	3.3
fat (adj)	2.1
feel well	3.3
festival (n)	2.3
film (*photography*) (n)	4.1
filter (n)	4.1
finally (adv)	1.4
finish (v)	1.1
fire (n)	3.1
fire department (n)	3.1
firefighter (n)	1.3
fireworks (n pl)	2.4
first (adv)	2.2
flame (n)	3.1
flat (adj)	4.2
flight (n)	2.2
flower shop (n)	2.2
follow (v)	1.3
for (*time*) (prep)	1.4
foreign (adj)	2.1
forest (n)	3C
fortune (n)	3.4
fresh (water) (adj)	1C
friendly (adj)	2.1
front (n)	2.3
full (of) (adj)	2.1
future (n)	4.2
game show (n)	4.4
garbage (n)	3C
genius (n)	4.4
gerund (n)	4.4
get up (v)	2.3
giant (adj)	1C
gift (n)	2.2
glasses (n pl)	1.3
good (at) (adj)	2.3
Good luck!	2.4
government (n)	3.1
grammar (n)	3C
grape (n)	2.4
greeting card (n)	2.4
ground (n)	3.3
guest (n)	2.2
guys (n pl)	2.2
gymnastics (n)	1.1
haircut (n)	2.2
hairdresser's (n)	2.2
happily (adv)	4.3
happy (adj)	1.4
Happy New Year!	2.4
harbor (n)	3C
hard (adv)	
1 = with force	3.3

2 = with effort	4.3
hat (n)	1.2
have fun	3.2
health (n)	1.3
heavy metal (n)	2.3
helicopter (n)	3.1
hill (n)	3.1
hip-hop (n)	2.3
hit (v)	3.3
hold hands	1.2
hole (n)	3.3
hotel (n)	1.4
How about ...?	1.1
How long?	2.1
huge (adj)	1C
hungrily (adv)	4.4
I'm kidding.	1.1
illness (n)	4.4
image (n)	4.1
imaginary (adj)	4.4
immediately (n)	2.2
important (adj)	1.4
in fact (adv	1C
in front of (prep)	2.2
industry (n)	1C
infinitive (n)	4.4
inside (prep)	2.2
instant (adj)	4.1
instead (adv)	4.1
interactive (adj)	1C
interested (in) (adj)	2.3
interesting (adj)	1C
Internet (n)	1.3
interview (v)	1.3
introduce (v)	4.2
invent (v)	3.1
invention (n)	4.2
iron (*metal*) (n)	3.3
jacket (n)	1.2
jazz (n)	2.1
jeans (n pl)	1.2
join (v)	1C
judge (n)	2.1
juggler (n)	1.2
karate (n)	1.1
land (v)	3.3
laptop (n)	1.3
large (adj)	2.1
last (v)	2.1
late (adv)	1.1
later (adj)	3.4
later (adv)	2.2
lazy (adj)	3.2
lead singer (n)	2.3
lentils (n pl)	2.4
life (pl lives) (n)	1.3
light (v)	2.4
listen up (v)	2.2
liter (l) (n)	1C
live (adj)	2.3
look forward to	1.4
loud (adj)	2.1
loudly (adv)	4.3

LP (long-playing record) (n)	4.2
magnetic (adj)	3.3
major (adj)	3.4
make a phone call	3.1
make a wish	2.4
make friends	2.3
make sense	4.3
manner (n)	4.3
marry (v)	3.1
mathematics (n)	4.1
medical (adj)	4.4
medicine (n)	2.2
meeting (n)	1.3
meteorite (n)	3.3
microphone (n)	1.3
middle-class (adj)	4.4
mind (I don't mind.) (v)	2.3
miss (v)	1.4
mix (v)	4.1
model (n)	1C
modern (adj)	2.1
morning (n)	1.4
movie (n)	1.1
movie star (n)	1C
MP3 player (n)	4.2
mud (n)	2.3
multimedia (adj)	3.2
murderer (n)	4.4
museum (n)	1C
music show (n)	4.4
music store (n)	3.2
musician (n)	1.3
mystery (n)	4.4
natural (adj)	1C
near (prep)	2.2
need (v)	4.3
nervous (adj)	4.3
nervously (adv)	4.3
network (n)	1.3
New Year's Eve	2.4
news show (n)	4.4
newsstand (n)	2.2
next (*time*) (adj)	3.4
next to (prep)	1.2
night (n)	2.1
noise (n)	3.3
noisy (adj)	2.1
nonsense (n)	3C
nonstop (adj)	2.1
noodles (n pl)	2.4
normally (adv)	4.3
noun (n)	4.4
novel (n)	3.4
novelist (n)	3.4
nurse (n)	1.3
office (n)	1.3
old (adj)	2.1
on time	2.3
once (adv)	2.2
online (adv)	1.1
open-air (adj)	2.3
ordinary (adj)	4.4
ourselves (pron)	4.3

Word List

outside (prep)	2.2	rehearse (v)	4.3	snow (n)	1C
over (prep)	2.2	relax (v)	1.4	soap (opera) (n)	4.4
overboard (n)	3.3	replace (v)	4.2	social networking site (n)	1.3
PA (personal assistant) (n)	1.3	report (v)	3.1	sofa (n)	3.3
pain (n)	3.3	reporter (n)	1.3	soon (adv)	3.4
pants (n pl)	1.2	rescue (v)	3.3	soul (music) (n)	2.3
parade (n)	2.1	rest (= others) (n pl)	2.2	sound (n)	3.1
parking lot (n)	3C	return (v)	3.4	soup (n)	2.4
part-owner (n)	3.4	rice (n)	2.4	space (n)	1C
party (n)	2.1	rich (adj)	3.4	space flight (n)	1C
password (n)	1.3	ride (n)	1C	spaceship (n)	3.3
patient (n)	4.4	rock (n)		spectacular (adj)	2.1
perform (v)	1.3	1 = music	2.3	speedboat (n)	3.3
performance (n)	3.4	2 = stone	3.3	spend time	3.2
permission (n)	1.3	rock singer (n)	1C	sports show (n)	4.4
phonograph (n)	4.2	rocket (n)	1C	spread (v)	3.1
photographer (n)	1.3	roof (n)	3.3	square (adj & n)	1C
pickpocket (n)	1C	rudely (adv)	4.3	stadium (n)	2.1
pilot (n)	1.3	rule (n)	4.4	stage (n)	2.3
pixel (n)	4.1	sad (adj)	4.3	stall (n)	2.1
plan (v)	3.1	sadly (adv)	4.3	stamp (n)	2.2
plane (n)	1.3	safe (adj)	2.1	stand (I can't stand …) (v)	2.3
play (n)	3.2	safety (n)	2.2	start (n)	2.4
playwright (n)	3.4	salsa (n)	2.3	stay up late	2.3
pocket (n)	1C	salt water (n)	1C	steep (adj)	3.2
poem (n)	3.4	samba (n)	2.1	stethoscope (n)	1.3
police station (n)	2.2	satire (n)	4.4	still (adv)	1.3
politely (adv)	4.3	scene (n)	4.3	street fair (n)	2.2
politician (n)	4.4	schoolboy (n)	3.3	street performer (n)	1C
pop (music) (n)	2.3	science fiction series (n)	4.4	strike (n)	3.3
popular (adj)	1C	screen (n)	4.1	strong (adj)	3.1
post office (n)	2.2	sea lion (n)	1.1	studio (n)	3.1
prefer (v)	4.2	security (n)	2.3	substitute (v)	4.4
preposition (n)	4.4	sell (v)	2.1	succeed (v)	4.4
press (v)	4.1	separate (adj)	1C	success (n)	3.4
pretty (adj)	4.4	series (n)	4.4	successful (adj)	4.4
primary color (n)	4.1	serious (adj)	4.4	suddenly (adv)	3.3
print (v)	3.1	setting (n)	4.4	suitcase (n)	2.4
prison (n)	4.4	shake hands	2.2	sunglasses (n pl)	1.2
process (n)	4.1	ship (n)	3.3	sunshine (n)	1.4
produce (v)	4.1	shirt (n)	1.2	supermarket (n)	2.2
pronoun (n)	4.4	shoe (n)	1.2	surf (the Web) (v)	1.2
properly (adv)	4.3	shorts (n pl)	1.2	survive (v)	3.3
public (adj)	3.4	show (n)	1C	suspension bridge (n)	1C
publish (v)	3.4	side (n)	1C	sweater (n)	1.2
punk (n)	2.3	sightseeing (n)	1C	sweatshirt (n)	1.2
quick (adj)	1.2	sign up (v)	1.3	system (n)	3.2
quickly (adv)	3.1	simple (adj)	1.3	T-shirt (n)	1.2
quiet (adj)	2.1	simulator (n)	1C	take a picture	1.3
quietly (adv)	4.3	sink (v)	3.3	take a tour/trip	1C
railroad (n)	3C	sit down (v)	3.1	take care of someone	2.2
rap (music) (n)	2.3	sitcom (n)	4.4	take place	4.4
rare (adj)	3.3	site (n)		talent show (n)	4.4
reach (v)	3.3	1 = website	1.3	talk show (n)	4.4
reality show (n)	4.4	2 = area of land	1C	tape (n)	4.2
recent (adj)	4.4	size (n)	2.1	tape recorder (n)	4.2
receptionist (n)	1.3	skirt (n)	1.2	taxi (n)	2.1
record (n & v)	4.2	sky (n)	1.4	teacher (n)	1.3
recover (v)	2.1	sleep (v)	2.3	techno (n)	2.3
red-hot (adj)	3.3	slowly (adv)	4.3	telephone (n)	2.2
reggae (n)	2.3	smart (adj)	4.4	tell a story	3.3
region (n)	2.1	smoke (n)	3.1	tell the truth	1.4
rehearsal (n)	4.3	sneaker (n)	1.2	temple (n)	3.2

tent (n)	2.3
text message (n)	1.3
theater (n)	1C
theme park (n)	1C
then (adv)	2.4
thief (n)	1.2
thin (adj)	1.2
thirstily (adv)	4.4
thought (n)	4.4
thriller (n)	4.4
throw (v)	2.4
thunder (n)	3.3
tiny (adj)	3.3
tired (adj)	3.2
ton (n)	2.3
top (n)	1.2
tour guide (n)	1.2
tower (n)	1C
tradition (n)	2.4
traditional (adj)	2.4
tragedy (n)	3.4
train (n)	3.3
train (v)	1C
transportation (n)	2.2
trash (n)	2.3
travel agency (n)	2.2
triangle (n)	1C
trouble (n)	4.1
tweet (n)	1.3
twice (adv)	2.2
umbrella (n)	1.2
under (prep)	1C
underwear (n)	2.4
unlike (n)	4.1
until (conj)	2.2
until (prep)	3.2
unusual (adj)	1C
username (n)	1.3
usual (as usual) (adj)	2.1
verb (n)	4.4
vet (n)	1.3
wait in line	2.3
waiter (n)	1.2
wallet (n)	1.2
warm (adj)	2.1
waterfall (n)	1C
wave (ocean) (n)	2.4
Web (n)	1.1
website (n)	1.3
well (adv)	4.3
well known (adj)	2.1
wet (adj)	1C
What about ...?	1.1
What else?	1.1
when (conj)	1C
Why not?	2.2
wide (adj)	1C
will (document) (n)	3.4
wine (n)	2.4
work hard	4.3
world (music) (n)	2.3
world-famous (adj)	1C
writer (n)	3.4
year (n)	1C
yoga (n)	1.1

CATEGORIES

This is a list of important categories covered in the book—for reference, and for active use when necessary.

ADVERBS OF MANNER

angrily (adv)	4.3
badly (adv)	3.1
carefully (adv)	4.3
easily (adv)	4.4
fast (adv)	3.3
happily (adv)	4.3
hard (adv)	3.3
hungrily (adv)	4.4
late (adv)	1.1
loudly (adv)	4.3
nervously (adv)	4.3
normally (adv)	4.3
politely (adv)	4.3
properly (adv)	4.3
quickly (adv)	3.1
quietly (adv)	4.3
rudely (adv)	4.3
sadly (adv)	4.3
slowly (adv)	4.3
thirstily (adv)	4.4
well (adv)	4.3

CLOTHES AND ACCESSORIES

bag (n)	1.2
camera (n)	1.2
clothes (n)	1.2
dress (n)	1.4
glasses (n pl)	1.3
hat (n)	1.2
jacket (n)	1.2
jeans (n pl)	1.2
pants (n pl)	1.2
pocket (n)	1C
shirt (n)	1.2
shoe (n)	1.2
shorts (n pl)	1.2
skirt (n)	1.2
sneaker (n)	1.2
sunglasses (n pl)	1.2
sweater (n)	1.2
sweatshirt (n)	1.2
top (n)	1.2
T-shirt (n)	1.2
umbrella (n)	1.2
underwear (n)	2.4
wallet (n)	1.2

COMMUNICATION TECHNOLOGY

account (n)	1.3
cell phone (n)	1.3
character (e.g. letter) (n)	1.3
e-mail address (n)	1.3
Internet (n)	1.3
laptop (n)	1.3
microphone (n)	1.3
network (n)	1.3
online (adv)	1.1

password (n)	1.3
sign up (v)	1.3
social networking site (n)	1.3
surf (the Web) (v)	1.2
text message (n)	1.3
tweet (n)	1.3
username (n)	1.3
Web (n)	1.1
website (n)	1.3

FEELINGS

afraid (of) (adj)	4.2
angry (adj)	1.4
happy (adj)	1.4
nervous (adj)	4.3
sad (adj)	4.3

FESTIVALS AND CELEBRATIONS

ball (= dance) (n)	2.1
candle (n)	2.4
carnival (n)	2.1
celebrate (v)	2.1
celebration (n)	2.4
Christmas	1C
costume (n)	2.1
dancer (n)	2.1
festival (n)	2.3
fireworks (n pl)	2.4
gift (n)	2.2
greeting card (n)	2.4
Happy New Year!	2.4
New Year's Eve	2.4
parade (n)	2.1
party (n)	2.1
stage (n)	2.3
street fair (n)	2.2

FOOD AND DRINK

burger (n)	2.3
champagne (n)	2.4
grape (n)	2.4
lentils (n pl)	2.4
noodles (n pl)	2.4
rice (n)	2.4
soup (n)	2.4
wine (n)	2.4

GRAMMAR WORDS

adjective (n)	4.4
adverb (n)	4.4
gerund (n)	4.4
grammar (n)	3C
infinitive (n)	4.4
noun (n)	4.4
preposition (n)	4.4
pronoun (n)	4.4
verb (n)	4.4

JOBS AND OCCUPATIONS

actor (n)	1.3
astronaut (n)	1C
businessman (n)	4.4
boss (n)	1.3
career (n)	3.4
doctor (n)	1.3
explorer (n)	3C

Word List

MUSIC... (see below — categorized listing)

firefighter (n) — 1.3
judge (n) — 2.1
juggler (n) — 1.2
lead singer (n) — 2.3
movie star (n) — 1C
musician (n) — 1.3
novelist (n) — 3.4
nurse (n) — 1.3
office (n) — 1.3
PA (personal assistant) (n) — 1.3
photographer (n) — 1.3
pilot (n) — 1.3
playwright (n) — 3.4
politician (n) — 4.4
receptionist (n) — 1.3
reporter (n) — 1.3
rock singer (n) — 1C
street performer (n) — 1C
teacher (n) — 1.3
tour guide (n) — 1.2
vet (n) — 1.3
waiter (n) — 1.2
writer (n) — 3.4

MUSIC

drummer (n) — 2.1
heavy metal (n) — 2.3
hip-hop (n) — 2.3
jazz (n) — 2.1
lead singer (n) — 2.3
pop (n) — 2.3
punk (n) — 2.3
rap (n) — 2.3
reggae (n) — 2.3
rock (n) — 2.3
salsa (n) — 2.3
samba (n) — 2.1
soul (n) — 2.3
techno (n) — 2.3
world (n) — 2.3

PERFORMANCE

acting company (n) — 3.4
actor (n) — 1.3
backstage (adv) — 2.3
band (n) — 1.3
character (person) (n) — 4.3
concert (n) — 4.3
costume (n) — 2.1
drama (n) — 4.3
director (n) — 4.3
episode (n) — 4.4
movie (n) — 1.1
musician (n) — 1.3
perform (v) — 1.3
performance (n) — 3.4
play (n) — 3.2
rehearsal (n) — 4.3
rehearse (v) — 4.3
scene (n) — 4.3
show (n) — 1C
stage (n) — 2.3
street performer (n) — 1C
studio (n) — 3.1
theater (n) — 1C

PHOTOGRAPHY

brightness (n) — 4.1
button (n) — 4.1
calculation (n) — 4.1
computer chip (n) — 4.1
digital photo (n) — 4.1
film (n) — 4.1
filter (n) — 4.1
image (n) — 4.1
pixel (n) — 4.1
primary color (n) — 4.1

PREPOSITIONS OF PLACE

across from (prep) — 2.2
behind (prep) — 1.2
between (prep) — 1C
in front of (prep) — 2.2
inside (prep) — 2.2
near (prep) — 2.2
next to (prep) — 1.2
outside (prep) — 2.2
over (prep) — 2.2
under (prep) — 1C

SOUND RECORDING

cassette (n) — 4.2
CD (compact disc) (n) — 4.2
cylinder (n) — 4.2
disc (n) — 4.2
LP (long playing record) (n) — 4.2
MP3 player (n) — 4.2
phonograph (n) — 4.2
record (n & v) — 4.2
tape (n) — 4.2
tape recorder (n) — 4.2

TIME REFERENCE WORDS

after (prep) — 1.1
afternoon (n) — 3.2
afterward (adv) — 3.3
ago (prep) — 3C
at first (adv) — 3.3
between (prep) — 3.2
by (prep) — 3.1
day (n) — 1.3
during (prep) — 2.1
early (adv) — 2.2
evening (n) — 1.4
finally (adv) — 1.4
first (adv) — 2.2
for (prep) — 1.4
in (prep) — 1.1
late (adv) — 1.1
later (adv) — 2.2
later (adj) — 3.4
morning (n) — 1.4
next (adj) — 3.4
night (n) — 2.1
on (prep) — 1.1
once (adv) — 2.2
recent (adj) — 4.4
soon (adv) — 3.4
still (adv) — 1.3
suddenly (adv) — 3.3
then (adv) — 2.4
twice (adv) — 2.2
until (conj) — 2.2
until (prep) — 3.2
when (conj) — 1C
year (n) — 1C

TOWN FACILITIES

bank (n) — 2.2
bookstore (n) — 2.2
cathedral (n) — 3.2
church (n) — 2.4
coffee shop (n) — 2.2
drugstore (n) — 2.2
fire department (n) — 3.1
flower shop (n) — 2.2
hairdresser's (n) — 2.2
hotel (n) — 1.4
music store (n) — 3.2
newsstand (n) — 2.2
parking lot (n) — 3C
police station (n) — 2.2
post office (n) — 2.2
stadium (n) — 2.1
supermarket (n) — 2.2
temple (n) — 3.2
theater (n) — 1C
travel agency (n) — 2.2

TOURIST ATTRACTIONS

aquarium (n) — 1C
canyon (n) — 1C
circus (n) — 1C
falls (n pl) — 1C
museum (n) — 1C
sightseeing (n) — 1C
suspension bridge (n) — 1C
theme park (n) — 1C
waterfall (n) — 1C

TRANSPORTATION

bicycle (n) — 3.3
boat (n) — 1C
bus (n) — 1C
cable car (n) — 2.2
car (n) — 3.1
flight (n) — 2.2
helicopter (n) — 3.1
plane (n) — 1.3
railroad (n) — 3C
rocket (n) — 1C
ship (n) — 3.3
spaceship (n) — 3.3
speedboat (n) — 3.3
taxi (n) — 2.1
train (n) — 3.3
transportation (n) — 2.2

TV SHOWS

broadcast (n) — 4.4
broadcast (v) — 1.3
cartoon (n) — 3.1
drama (n) — 4.4
documentary (n) — 4.4
game show (n) — 4.4
music show (n) — 4.4
news show (n) — 4.4
reality show (n) — 4.4
science fiction series (n) — 4.4
sitcom (n) — 4.4
soap (opera) (n) — 4.4
sports show (n) — 4.4
talent show (n) — 4.4
talk show (n) — 4.4
thriller (n) — 4.4

Pronunciation Guide

VOWELS

/i/	s<u>ee</u>, happ<u>y</u>		/u/	f<u>oo</u>d, tw<u>o</u>
/ɪ/	g<u>i</u>ve, d<u>i</u>d		/ə/	<u>a</u>bout, yog<u>a</u>
/e/	b<u>e</u>d, h<u>ea</u>d		/ɜr/	b<u>ir</u>d, h<u>ear</u>d
/æ/	b<u>a</u>d, c<u>a</u>p		/eɪ/	d<u>ay</u>, r<u>ai</u>n
/ɑ/	f<u>a</u>ther, h<u>o</u>t		/aɪ/	r<u>i</u>de, fl<u>y</u>
/ɔ/	b<u>ou</u>ght, t<u>a</u>lk		/ɔɪ/	p<u>oi</u>nt, b<u>oy</u>
/ʌ/	f<u>u</u>n, c<u>o</u>me		/oʊ/	c<u>o</u>ld, b<u>oa</u>t
/ʊ/	f<u>oo</u>t, c<u>ou</u>ld		/aʊ/	h<u>ow</u>, m<u>ou</u>th

CONSONANTS

/b/	<u>b</u>ag, ra<u>bb</u>it		/s/	<u>s</u>ay, thi<u>s</u>
/d/	<u>d</u>esk, col<u>d</u>		/t/	<u>t</u>own, ci<u>t</u>y
/f/	<u>f</u>ill, lau<u>gh</u>		/v/	<u>v</u>ery, li<u>v</u>e
/g/	<u>g</u>irl, bi<u>g</u>		/w/	<u>w</u>ater, a<u>w</u>ay
/h/	<u>h</u>and, <u>h</u>ome		/z/	<u>z</u>oo, hi<u>s</u>
/j/	<u>y</u>es, <u>y</u>oung		/ʃ/	<u>sh</u>op, ma<u>ch</u>ine
/k/	<u>c</u>ook, ba<u>ck</u>		/ʒ/	u<u>s</u>ually, televi<u>s</u>ion
/l/	<u>l</u>ike, fi<u>ll</u>		/ŋ/	tha<u>n</u>k, doi<u>ng</u>
/m/	<u>m</u>ean, cli<u>mb</u>		/tʃ/	<u>ch</u>eese, pic<u>t</u>ure
/n/	<u>n</u>ew, wa<u>n</u>t		/θ/	<u>th</u>ing, nor<u>th</u>
/p/	<u>p</u>ark, ha<u>pp</u>y		/ð/	<u>th</u>at, clo<u>th</u>es
/r/	<u>r</u>ing, bo<u>rr</u>ow		/dʒ/	<u>j</u>eans, bri<u>dg</u>e

Irregular Verbs

Infinitive	Simple past	Infinitive	Simple past	Infinitive	Simple past
be	was, were	go	went	see	saw
become	became	hang	hung	sell	sold
begin	began	have	had	send	sent
bite	bit	hear	heard	shine	shone
bring	brought	hide	hid	sing	sang
broadcast	broadcast	hit	hit	sink	sank/sunk
build	built	hold	held	sit	sat
buy	bought	hurt	hurt	sleep	slept
catch	caught	keep	kept	speak	spoke
choose	chose	know	knew	spend	spent
come	came	leave	left	spread	spread
cost	cost	lend	lent	stand	stood
cut	cut	let	let	steal	stole
dive	dived/dove	light	lit/lighted	swim	swam
do	did	lose	lost	take	took
draw	drew	make	made	teach	taught
drink	drank	mean	meant	tell	told
drive	drove	meet	met	think	thought
eat	ate	pay	paid	throw	threw
fall	fell	put	put	understand	understood
feel	felt	read /rid/	read /red/	wake	woke
find	found	rewrite	rewrote	wear	wore
fly	flew	ride	rode	win	won
forget	forgot	ring	rang	write	wrote
get	got	run	ran		
give	gave	say	said		

Macmillan Education
4 Crinan Street
London N1 9XW
A division of Springer Nature Limited
Companies and representatives throughout the world

ISBN 978-0-230-43414-1

Designed by The Write People
Cover design by The Write People
Cover Images courtesy of Alamy/Ambient Images, Digital Stock

The authors and publishers would like to thank the following to reproduce
their artwork:
Adrian Barclay pp 77-78; **Mark Brierley** pp 93, 107r;
Mark Davis pp107l, 120; **Mark Duffin** p 84;Tim Kahane pp 89, 110, 114;
Bill Piggins p 102; **Martin Sanders** pp 22 and 27;
Nadine Wickenden pp 45, 47 and 65; **and Gary Wing** pp 98, 101.

The author and publishers would like to thank the following for permission to
reproduce their photographs:
Alamy/Amana Images p30(C), Alamy/Ambient Images pp50, 84(bl),
Alamy/Greg Balfour Evans p41(cr), Alamy/Todd Bannor pp10(background),
11(Background), p45(tr), 76 (background), Alamy/CBW p113(4), Alamy/A
Chaderros/Onoky p63, Alamy/Tony Cordoza p7(1, 2), Alamy/DK p43(C
background), Alamy/Ian Dagnall p42(B background), Alamy/Michael De Freita
& North America pp4, 5(background), Alamy/Doyeol (David) p12(Theresa)
Alamy/David R Frasier Photolibrary Inc p43(D background), Alamy/Damien
P.Gadal pp22(E), 26(background), Alamy/Juice Images p51(4), Alamy/LHB
Photo p18(3), Alamy/Stephen May pp22(d), 28(background), 29, Alamy/
Motoring Picture Library pp41(benz), 49(tr), Alamy/Nagelstock p30(B), Alamy/
Neibrugge Images p84(tr), Alamy/RN Novosti p32(br), Alamy/Mauritius Images
GmbH p88(tr), Alamy/Steven May p90, Alamy/Mervyn Rees p19(8), Alamy/

Photoalto p12(Luke), Alamy/The Print Collector p48(t), Alamy/Friedrich Saurer
p35(B), 45, Alamy/Johnny Stockshooter p19(9), Alamy/Todd Bannor p45(tr),
76 background, Alamy/Worldwide Photo p12(Anna); **Bananastock** p56(tl,tr),
57(on phone); **BrandX** p23(2), 55(br), 87(bb), 95; **CEN**/Europics p38(A), 44,
45(bl),49(cl); **Corbis** p64(tr), 108(l, cr), Corbis/Morton Beebe p84(bc), Corbis/
Blaine Harrington III p84(br), Corbis/So Hing Keung pp30(E), 36, Corbis/
Cedric Lim/Asia Pix p12(Bill), Corbis/George Logan pp22(c), 24, 25, Corbis/
Tannen Maury/epa p87(btl), Corbis/Tazetra Images p96, Corbis/Olix Wirtlinger
pp54, 59(5), Corbis/Kelly Redinger/Design Pics p43(cr); **Comstock** p50(3);
Stuart Cox pp4(foreground characters), 5 (foreground characters), 7(3, 5, 6),
8(all),9(characters), 14(bl, br), 15, 17(bl), 26, 54(A),55(1-6), 60, 61, 70, 71,
74, 75, 76(cut outs), 80, 83, 88(b all); **Digital Stock** pp18(4), 100; **Digital
Vision** p55(3); **Getty** pp16(tl), 18(2), 22(b), 23(3), 29(insert), 55(4), 78(Teri,
Isabella, Mark Clarke), 108(br), 113(3), Getty/Bloomberg p42(A), Getty/David
Clapp pp8(r), 9(tl), 17(cr), 49(tr). 18(1), Getty/George Doyle pp12(Rosie),
84(tc), Getty/Alan Everard p30(F), Getty/Don Farrall p113(2), Getty/Jeff J
Mitchell p92, Getty/Moment p68, Getty/Marvin E Newman p85(background),
Getty/Caroline Purser p112(br), Getty/SSPL pp41(bcl, tr), Getty Steve Shott
p41(br), Getty/Johnny Stock Shooter p31, Getty/Superstock p38(C), 40, Getty/
Tetra Images p12(Scott); **Image Source** pp19(7), 23(bl), 41(biro), 55(1),
64(tc), 78(Val), 84(tl), 108(r), 109(t,insert); **Springer Nature** p55(2),
78(Anthony), Macmillan Australia p56(bl), 113(5), Macmillan Education/
Paul Bricknall p23(5), Macmillan Education/Haddon Davis p7(4), Macmillan
Education/Dean Ryan p57(camera, phone); **Mary Evans Picture Library**
pp51(cr,br), 58(1, 2); **North Devon Journal** p102; **Photoalto** p23(6);
Photodisc/Getty pp23(1, 4), 55(5, 6, bl), 110(bl,c); **Photoshot**/Imagebrokers
p32(cr), Photoshot/WPN p30(A), 32(tr); **Rex Features**/20th Century Fox/
Everett pp46(tr), 62(A, D), 65(cr), 116, 119, Rex Features/ABC/Everett p62(C),
64(cr), Rex Features/CBS Everett p115, Rex Features/Alex J Berliner/BEI p33,
Rex Features/CBS/Everett p62(B), Rex Features/Columbia Everett p47(b),
Rex Features/Robert Hallam p11(juggler), Rex Features/Ken McKay p64(tl),
Rex Features/Dean Murray p28(bl), Rex Features/ Elma Okic p112(cr), Rex
Features/Pekka Sakki p41(phone); **Robert Harding**/Alain Evrad p86; **Science
and Society** pp41(helicopter, bl), 113(1); **Stockbyte** p16(tr); **Superstock**
pp46(bl), 47(t), 49(br), 87(btr), 108(cl), Superstock/Age Fotostock p30(D);
Westcountryphotographers.com p99

These materials may contain links for third-party websites. We have no control
over, and are not responsible for, the contents of such third-party websites.
Please use care when accessing them.

While every effort has been made to locate the owners of copyright material
in this book, there may have been some cases when the publishers have been
unable to contact the owners. We should be grateful to hear from anyone
who recognizes copyright material and who is unacknowledged. We shall be
pleased to make the necessary amendments in future editions of the book.

Printed and bound in Lebanon

2018
11